W9-AYD-709

Straight Talk About Drugs and Alcohol

Straight Talk About Drugs and Alcohol

Elizabeth A. Ryan

362.2
Rya

18302

Facts On File
New York · Oxford

Straight Talk About Drugs and Alcohol

Copyright © 1989 by Elizabeth A. Ryan

All rights reserved. No part of this book may
be reproduced or utilized in any form or by any
means, electronic or mechanical, including
photocopying, recording, or by any information
storage and retrieval systems, without permission
in writing from the publisher.

Library of Congress Cataloging-in-Publication Data

Ryan, Elizabeth A. (Elizabeth Anne), 1943-
Straight talk about drugs and alcohol / Elizabeth A. Ryan.
p. cm.
Includes index.
Summary: Discusses the physical and social effects of drug and
alcohol abuse, how to recognize an addiction, and how to get help
for a dependency problem.
ISBN 0-8160-1525-2
1. Teenagers—United States—Drug use—Juvenile literature.
2. Teenagers—United States—Alcohol use—Juvenile literature.
3. Drug abuse—United States—Prevention—Juvenile literature.
4. Alcoholism—United States—Prevention—Juvenile literature.
[1. Drug abuse. 2. Alcoholism.] I. Title.
HV5824.Y68R93 1988
362.2'92—dc19 88-18050

British CIP data available on request

Printed in the United States of America

10 9 8 7 6 5 4 3 2 1

Contents

Preface

Another book on drugs and alcohol? Yes, but this one is different because it gives you information that you may not have seen anywhere else. You'll find out exactly what drugs and alcohol can do: how they make you feel, how you can become addicted, and how you can get off them if you need to. You'll also find out why people turn to drugs and alcohol: what makes one person depend on them for "survival" while another is indifferent to their effects.

The use of drugs and the abuse of alcohol are serious problems, but the only way you can reasonably explore solutions is with balanced, comprehensive information. This book won't tell you what you can and can't do; it will, however, give you the facts so that you can make choices that are right for you. By finding out what you need to know, you can see the problems that drugs and alcohol can cause. You will also see that you aren't alone in looking for answers to your own problems. Most of all you'll find out that there are solutions and that there is help if you need it.

Acknowledgments

Many thanks for the generous assistance of the following groups and individuals, without whom this book would not have been possible: Alcoholics Anonymous, Daytop Village, Fair Oaks Hospital, Freedom Institute Inc., the National Institutes of Alcoholism and Alcohol Abuse, and Dr. Dorienne Sorter.

My deepest thanks go also to James Warren, one of the best and most patient editors I've known, and to John Thornton, one of the most intelligent men in publishing.
E.R.

Straight Talk About Drugs and Alcohol

1

The
Addictive Society

Theoretically, this society does not approve of teenagers using alcohol. And it doesn't approve of anyone using illegal drugs. Legal drugs—caffeine, tranquilizers, diet pills—encompass a kind of gray area, and are generally considered acceptable for both teens and adults, with some exceptions. In practice, however, the messages you get about what is and isn't permissible are usually mixed. If it's OK to drink three or four cups of coffee to stay up late the night before an exam, why isn't it OK to take speed for the same purpose? If your parents don't want you to drink, why is it OK for them? If marijuana isn't acceptable at your parties, why is cocaine acceptable at Hollywood bashes?

If you've thought about drugs and drinking at all, you've probably come to the conclusion that what people say and what they actually do are often very different. This difference may have puzzled you, or worried you, or made you angry. After all, how are you supposed to know what to do when you are getting mixed messages?

There may be another reason for your reactions, as well. The more you understand that adults are giving you mixed messages, the clearer it becomes that you are going to have to decide the difficult issue of drug and alcohol use for yourself.

You are going to have to come up with your own rules about what makes sense, what feels safe, what kind of behavior you respect. And that's hard. It's always easier to face a situation where there are clear rules that everybody can agree to. Even if you break those rules, at least you know what kind of response your behavior is likely to elicit. With drugs and alcohol, you don't have that comfort. Even if you eventually decide that you are in complete agreement with the rules of your parents or your school, you are going to have to come to this conclusion for yourself—for your own reasons—and you are going to have to be prepared for the possibility that *someone* may disagree with *whatever* decision you make.

The good news is that it's much more satisfying in the end to make your own decisions. You'll feel stronger, surer of yourself, and better prepared to make the other difficult decisions that you'll be facing as an adult. For the rest of your life, you'll confront situations where you receive conflicting messages, where people disagree, where what you were taught at home is challenged by people you meet. Making the right decisions *is* often difficult and scary—but it can also be exciting and empowering.

Approaching the Subject of Drugs and Alcohol

As you try to think this problem through, it will help to have the most complete information possible about what drugs and alcohol are, how they affect you, and how they are used. It will also help to know what other teenagers are thinking, to realize that you are not alone in making decisions about drugs and alcohol. This book will try to give you the information you need, and to give you some ways to think about the problem.

As you think about your own feelings toward drugs and alcohol, you may feel that you're getting a lot of messages that say that drugs are OK for some people but not for you. Every time a movie star or a star athlete dies of a drug overdose, the papers are full of stories about the wild parties where drugs are as common as potato chips. Stories of Wall Street traders using cocaine to make it through their high-pressure days seem to accompany news reports of big drug busts. And of course, there are all the "legal" drugs—over-the-counter or prescription painkillers, diet pills, and tranquilizers; coffee; and the cigarettes and alcohol that are legal for adult users but not for you.

It's certainly true that many adults take drugs, and that even more adults drink. Although the number of regular cocaine users seems to have peaked in the late 1970s, at about 5 million, individual coke consumption is up, so that there's been an 11 percent increase in the drug's total use. Heroin consumption has decreased—there are now about 500,000 heroin addicts in the U.S., 200,000 of them in New York City—and so has the consumption of marijuana. But the marijuana being sold today is more potent than the drug of 10 or 15 years ago. And other types of illegal drugs, such as angel dust/PCP, have become more common, so that the total use of illegal drugs has increased by over 15 percent in the past few years.

However many people take illegal drugs, it's just a drop in the bucket compared to the number of people having problems with alcohol. The National Council on Alcoholism estimates that if you divided the total alcohol consumed in this country by the number of people over the age of 14, it would work out that everyone was drinking the equivalent of 2.7 gallons of pure alcohol every year. That's roughly 591 12-ounce cans of beer, 215 bottles of table wine, or 35 bottles of 80-proof whiskey a year. Of course, some people drink far less than that—so, to account for the average, some people drink far, far more. One-twentieth of the drinking population drinks half the alcoholic beverages sold.

Adults are also abusing "legal" drugs, such as Valium, which is one of the most often prescribed drugs in the country. In recognition of the growing problem with Valium and several other tranquilizers (such as Ativan, Dalmane, Librium, and Centrax), New York State recently tightened up its reporting procedures for doctors. Many women's health activists have complained that doctors over-prescribe tranquilizers and sedatives for their patients, especially for their women patients, rather than helping them to find other ways of dealing with their mental or physical problems.

This heavy use of drugs and alcohol has its price. There are the obvious costs: debt, death, disease, imprisonment. There are now about 600 cocaine-related deaths per year, with the number expected to increase as the use of crack spreads across the country. A recent study of teenage suicides found that teen suicide rates had increased over the years, and that more teen suicides were linked to drugs and alcohol. According to National Institutes of Health statistics, over a 20-year period, the number of 15-to-19-year-old suicides rose from 3.7 per 100,000 to 8.7 per 100,000. During roughly the same period, the percent of teen suicides committed while the person was drunk or high rose from 3.4 percent to 31 percent. Alcohol kills about 98,000 people each year, almost 50,000 of whom die in auto accidents. The Drug Enforcement Administration—the federal agency that handles drug-related crime—is averaging 41 arrests per day, an increase of 18 percent over the past two years.

As the society tries to deal with these problems, we begin to see the more subtle costs of abuse. It was recently revealed that in one Silicon Valley company, 90 percent of the firm's 400 employees were using drugs. Alarmed by the potential costs of absenteeism and losses in productivity, more and more companies have begun instituting some form of employee drug testing. Currently, almost one-third of the *Fortune* 500 companies have such tests. Many people strongly oppose these tests, claiming that they are an invasion of privacy and an attack on the dignity of employees. Many critics also challenge the reliability of drug testing. Even those who support such tests regret the atmosphere of suspicion and distrust that they promote.

Drug tests have also become more common in schools, raising related questions about whether or not schools have the right to search student lockers, or to bar students from school activities on the basis of test results. Students familiar with such stories as that of the Florida teacher arrested for snorting cocaine at his desk while showing his students a biology film resent what they see as the hypocrisy and intrusive nature of the tests. Other students feel victimized by drug-related crime, or pressured by the widespread use of drugs among their peers. They hope that punishments and tests will turn their schools into drug-free environments.

In an atmosphere where there are so many mixed messages about drugs, it's hard to make good choices about them. On the one hand, politicians and TV reporters make it seem as if "the drug problem" were the biggest crisis facing the country. The National Council on Alcoholism claims that alcohol, not drugs, is the number-one problem for teens, estimating that in 1985 alone, some 4.6 million young people between the ages of 14 and 17 suffered negative consequences from drinking: arrests, accidents, health problems, and poor job performance. In the same year, some 10,000 people ages 16 to 24 were killed in alcohol-related accidents, including drowning, suicides, homicides, violent injuries, and fires. Teens with drug-related problems number in the thousands, or perhaps the hundred thousands—teens with alcohol-related problems number in the millions. Yet the very TV press conference or news special on the dangers of crack may be interspersed with commercials for beer or wine.

Meanwhile, the federal government steps up enforcement procedures while cutting funds for treatment centers. In Florida's Dade County, only one addict in 10 can find a place in a treatment program. There are over 1,000 people on waiting lists for residential centers in New York City; Los Angeles's Watts Clinic has only 29 beds and a waiting list of 200. In Texas, the budget for drug-treatment programs was recently cut by almost one-fifth; federal block grants for drug programs have gone down by 40 percent since 1980.

Likewise, school officials denounce drugs, but, as Jesse Jackson recently pointed out, some teachers and security guards even sell drugs to their students. And if TV ads make it seem that happy, attractive people are drinking coffee to wake up, taking diet pills to stop eating, and using pain-relievers to cope with the tension in their high-stress jobs, then what could possibly be wrong with relying on chemical substances to help you get through your life?

The question is not whether or not some people in the society are putting out mixed messages about how bad drugs and alcohol are. The problem is not that some adults seem to follow a policy of "Do as I say, not as I do." The decision you face is not whether you find their behavior hypocritical or dishonest. The real question is not for them: how might taking drugs and drinking alcohol affect your life?

The Teen Factor

You might begin to sort this difficult question out by thinking about the stage of life you're in. Adolescence—the teenage years—is a tough time. Despite the phrase "the best years of your life," the years between 13 and 19 are probably some of the most difficult times you'll ever have to go through. These years can also be exciting, full of intense feeling, very high "highs" and very low "lows." That's because adolescence is a time of change—physical, social, mental, and emotional change. And change is never easy.

On a physical level, your body is changing in obvious and not-so-obvious ways. Your physical development into adulthood involves hormonal changes in your body chemistry. These changes eventually settle down, but during the growth spurts of these years, you may experience mysterious mood swings, depression, irritability, or, sometimes, an unexplained sense of euphoria and power.

Because you are in a time of change, you are experiencing many things for the first time. Feelings of love, or physical desire, may overtake you in ways quite different from what you experienced as a 10- or 11-year-old. Worries about the future, about the kind of work you want to do or the kind of person you want to be, go along with your new realization that you will be on your own in just a few years. Issues of love, work, identity, will continue to be important to you throughout your whole life. No one ever completely "solves" these problems; the problems only change as your life changes. But as a teenager, you are facing many of these problems for the first time. That may make them seem extra difficult. It certainly means that they take more time and energy to deal with. And because you haven't been through these problems before, you may feel that you're trapped inside them, that there's no way out.

As you move through your teenage years, you may feel that you are getting it from both ends. On the one hand, you are beginning to challenge things that you used to take for granted. You have new feelings to put into place. You're beginning to question the values you were raised with, to ask yourself what kind of a person you want to be. On the other hand, just at this time when everything seems so uncertain, you are faced with new responsibilities that seem to demand even more of you. Your parents may expect you to contribute to the household financially, or to take on new housework or childcare responsibilities. Your schoolwork is suddenly playing a major role in your future, as it determines where or even whether you can go on to college or some other post-secondary program. Friends, boyfriends, or girlfriends may be making new demands upon you, seeking your advice or emotional support for their life crises. You may have to handle a difficult balancing act: figuring out who you are while meeting new and difficult demands.

One of the most complicated tasks you face during your teenage years is working out a new relationship to your parents. Adolescence is a time for figuring out who *you* are—that may mean disagreeing with your parents, or finding ways to break away from them. Developing your own sense of independence doesn't have to mean defying your parents at every turn, or saying "black" every time they say "white." But avoiding knee-jerk negative reactions to your parents can be difficult sometimes, especially because you are not used to seeing your parents as people with problems of their own, who may need things from you just as you need things from them. You've never been a teenager before, but your parents may have never been parents of a teenager before, and the situation takes some adjusting for both of you. You may be torn between wanting to believe that your parents can still take care of you and wanting to believe that you don't need them any more. They may welcome your growing independence while feeling sad or guilty that they're unable to protect you any longer. All these very real conflicts affect your thinking as you try to decide how you feel about your parents' rules for drinking and drug use.

In the midst of these conflicting pressures, many teens have turned to drinking or drug taking as a way out. You may feel that defying your parents' rules in this area is a way of exploring independence. You might feel that drinking dissolves your worries, or that getting high makes you feel like the powerful person you wish you really were. Drinking or drugs might be such a big part of your friends' social life that anyone who doesn't go along with the party is left out. Or you might just feel that getting high is fun, a pleasant way to pass the time.

The challenge for you as you think about this issue is to make sure that *you* are the most important person in your thoughts—not your parents, not your friends. Even if your parents have what seem like silly rules about drugs and drinking, that doesn't guarantee that doing the exact opposite of what your parents want will be what *you* want. For example, your parents may say that only juvenile delinquents take drugs, and that's why they don't want you to take them. You may decide from your own experience that you do not agree—you know plenty of drug-takers who are clearly not "juvenile delinquents." You may even be excited or happy about having found a place where your parents are so clearly wrong. But even if they *are* wrong, does that mean that you are declaring your independence from them by taking drugs? If you rush to do exactly the opposite of what your parents want, you are not really independent from them. Their rules are still guiding your actions, whether you are following those rules or breaking them.

Conflicts and disagreements with your parents are a natural part of being a teenager. The challenge is to take the disagreement all the way—to the place where you are really thinking through what is right for you, not what is wrong for your parents. And if you end up agreeing with your parents, when in general you don't—well, you might enjoy *not* having to fight with them!

Another important teenage experience is making friends who may have different values from your parents'. But again, you need to make sure that you don't transfer authority from your parents to your friends. Learning to disagree with people and still be close to them is part of growing up. Again, the challenge is to decide how you can do what is best for you, rather than worrying about pleasing other people. You need friends who will help you feel secure and good about yourself, not those who make you worry constantly about whether they'll drop you if you disagree with them.

If you are turning to drugs or drinking as a way to feel more powerful, or as the main way to have a good time, you might want to look at the *whole* experience of drinking and drugs. Do you enjoy having a hangover or getting sick? Do you feel powerful wondering how you're going to pay for the drugs you want—or feel you need? Do you feel powerful feeling that you need drugs or liquor to have a good time, or to make it through the school day, or to face a difficult situation? Once again, you need to think about what is satisfying to *you*. If you find some parts of your experience with drugs or drinking satisfying but other parts upsetting, boring, or painful, think about how *all* the parts of your experience affect your life. Think about what really works for you and what doesn't, so that you can make a real choice.

Although when most people say "drugs," they mean "illegal drugs," it's true that there are lots of legal drugs in this society as well. Many people see nothing wrong with drinking a cup of coffee to wake up in the morning, or smoking a cigarette to relax. But the mind-active qualities of caffeine or nicotine exact a price—just as the high of alcohol or marijuana or crack does. Each drug has a different effect: different physical effects in the short-term and the long-term; different impact on your ability to function while driving, taking a test, or socializing; different rates of physical or psychological addiction. As you make your decisions about whether you want to drink or take illegal drugs, you may be tempted to compare them to legal drugs, or to argue that there's no difference, or to point out that "everybody does something."

All of those arguments may be true. But when it comes down to your own decisions about what is right for *you*, they're really beside the point. What you have to decide is what chemicals you want to take into your body, what long- and short-term physical dangers you're willing to risk, and what kind of life you want to lead. It will be up to you to figure out the difference between drinking a beer or two now and then and leading a social life that's entirely organized around drinking. You're the one who will be responsible for telling the difference between smoking one joint of marijuana (causes short-term memory loss, with possible long-term impact; seriously impairs driving ability; possible damage to menstrual cycle or sperm production; possible "psychological" addiction if user continues to smoke heavily or often) and smoking one hit of crack (sudden rise in blood pressure; heartbeat up 30 percent to 50 percent with high risk of heart attack; potential to become strongly physically addicted within two or three uses, leading to a recovery period averaging two years). Regardless of how you feel about the rules your parents make, or what you see them doing, you still have to assume responsibility for figuring out the kind of life you want for yourself. It's up to you to understand the difference between an interesting experiment and what could be a major risk; between an occasional drink or joint and a full-fledged addiction; between what everyone else does and what you want to do.

There are many ways that people try to handle pressures or worries that seem too much for them. Some people use drinking or drugs in this way. Other people find themselves eating compulsively. Sometimes people try to avoid their problems by involving themselves in a difficult or demanding relationship, or by falling in love with one unavailable person after another. Some people seek compulsively to socialize, frantically avoiding any time to be alone; other people withdraw, letting their anxiety keep them away from any human contact.

Many kinds of behavior that are all right in moderation are not all right when conducted compulsively or exclusively. Once in a while that hot fudge sundae does make you feel better. Sometimes buying something nice for yourself, going to a party, or just taking out an afternoon to be sad and lonely is the best thing you can do for yourself. In all of these cases, the in-dividual behavior might not be as important as the judgment

that supports it. If you know you're violently allergic to chocolate and will break out in a dark, ugly rash for days, even one hot
fudge might be too much. If your impulse to purchase turns
into a $200 shopping spree every time, your method of coping
probably isn't working.

Judgment is very important as you decide what your rules are
for drinking and drugs, as well. Some people cannot handle any
alcohol at all, unable to control their drinking once they've
begun. Others may find that traveling in a crowd that drinks or
does drugs means that their entire social life revolves around
getting high. And regardless of your abilities in other areas, you
almost certainly will not be able to handle crack or heroin,
which are highly physically addictive after even two or three
uses.

There are two steps to using your own judgment:

1. Look at the *whole* picture, as objectively as you can. What
   happens before you drink or take drugs? Do you feel
   nervous or anxious about a situation and turn to getting
   high as a way to cope? Do you have to spend a lot of time
   and trouble getting the money for the drugs or liquor, or
   getting hold of the drugs or liquor themselves? What
   happens during the time that you are getting high? How
   do you act? Who are you with? What is *not* happening that
   might be happening if you were straight? For example,
   does getting high at a party mean that you don't have to
   talk to people? Does getting high in school mean that you
   don't pay attention to the teacher? What about afterwards?
   What are the consequences of your drinking and using
   drugs?
2. Look at *all* of your feelings about the situation. Look at the
   good feelings as well as the bad ones, about all the facts
   that you have put together in thinking about before, during, and after using drugs or alcohol. Often people
   separate an experience into the good part, which they
   want to keep, and the bad part, which they would like to
   get rid of. One way of "getting rid of" the bad part is to
   pretend it doesn't happen, to "forget" about the hangover,
   or about the fact that you didn't make such a good impres-

sion on that new kid when you got drunk at that party, or about the way you felt even more shy or nervous or upset the next day when you were straight again.

If you can look at all of your behavior, all of the situation, and all of your feelings about it and still feel comfortable with your judgment, you know you are doing what is right for you. If you feel uncomfortable about any part of your actions or your feelings, you may want to examine your decision again.

Making decisions about drugs and alcohol isn't easy in a society that gives out mixed messages. And making any decision is difficult during adolescence, a time when everything seems open to question. But the more you know about yourself, and about drugs and alcohol, the better you will be able to make healthy and safe decisions and figure out how to stick to them.

2

Everybody's Doing It . . . Or Are They?

When you think about drug and alcohol use, you may feel as though everybody's doing it—or at least, everyone but you. Whether or not you use drugs or alcohol yourself, you may feel isolated as you try to decide how you feel about their use and as you think about the ways in which you'd like to relate to drugs and alcohol. It may seem as though there's only one way to think about drinking and getting high, or only two black-and-white choices.

In fact, drug and alcohol use has changed a great deal over the past 30 years, especially among teenagers. It's important for you to know that there never was just one pattern for either drinking or doing drugs: class, race, geography, age, and many other factors affected people's attitudes toward whether they wanted to drink; which—if any—drugs they considered using; and how they felt about others who drank or did drugs. In addition, social attitudes about both drugs and young people have changed several times.

As you think about your decision, it may help to look at the problem from a wider perspective. Knowing something about the history of teenage drug use, and about the current statistics on drugs and drinking, may help you to think more clearly about the decisions you want to make.

A Look at Teenage Drug and Alcohol Use

In the mid-1950s, drugs were not considered a very serious problem in the United States and teenage drug use was almost an unknown occurrence. Heroin was the drug that raised the most concern, but it was used by only about 65,000 people, mainly adults, living either in New York City or in other inner-city areas. Marijuana was associated either with jazz musicians, writers, and artists, or again with inner-city residents and Southwestern migrant workers. Cocaine was almost an unknown substance. And since the drugs that were used were associated primarily with Black and Latin inner-city residents, it was possible for the primarily white politicians and media to disregard the problem. And so they did.

In the early 1960s, the idea of a "youth culture" first began to emerge. For the first time, teenagers and young people were seen as a separate group with its own culture, a culture that included the use of drugs like marijuana, LSD, and other hallucinogens. Suddenly, drugs were not only associated with inner-city residents and criminals, but also with middle-class white teenagers with good economic and educational prospects. Drugs were also associated with many of the political attitudes that came out of the 1960s, such as a mistrust of authority and the desire to find other values than making money and fitting into corporate and professional life. Before the '60s, some people had argued for treating drug users with more tolerance, but the 1960s were the first time large groups of people were saying that drug use was actually a good thing.

It's interesting that during this period, the use of heroin was down among Black and Latin inner-city youth. Perhaps the hope and energy generated by the Civil Rights movement and the Chicano movement affected the decisions of teenagers in Black and Latin communities. At the same time, many young white men were becoming addicted to heroin in Vietnam and in many U.S. cities. For a while, it looked as though drug-use patterns in the U.S. were becoming more similar among different groups. Low-income youth from all races were affected by the counterculture; middle-class teens felt the impact of the Vietnam War.

In the 1970s, the number of young people arrested for illegal drug use went way up. This probably had something to do both with increased drug use and with the government's attitudes at the time, which favored "law and order" and criticized the politics of the antiwar "youth culture." Since 1973, drug arrests for white teenagers have steadily decreased, with ever bigger decreases in the 1980s. Meanwhile, the arrests for Black and Hispanic youth have stayed about the same, while arrests for Black and Latin adults have increased. It isn't clear whether these figures reflect differences in drug use or just differences in police attitudes towards these groups. In any case, a quarter of a million teens are still arrested for drug use each year.

In either case, one thing is clear: drug use has declined markedly since the 1970s. And it's gone down even faster in the 1980s than it did the decade before. In the late 1970s, for example, 37 percent of the teens surveyed said they had used marijuana sometime in the past month, and 11 percent said that they used it daily. In the mid-1980s, only 25 percent of the teens had smoked pot in the past month, with only 5 percent reporting a daily use. Sedatives, tranquilizers, inhalants, and hallucinogens have all declined in use since 1975. The use of cocaine and other stimulants has increased, but seems to be leveling off.

Clearly, many teenagers continue to experiment with both legal and illegal drugs. But recent surveys suggest both that fewer kids are experimenting, and that more teens who once took drugs are now quitting. The highest figure for "current use of an illegal drug"—use of that drug within the past month—was 39 percent of all high school students in 1979. In the early 1980s, that figure had already begun to drop, down to only 32 percent by 1983. In the same period of time, the figures on use of an illegal drug within the past year had dropped from 54 percent to only 49 percent.

Much of this decline is due to the ongoing drop in the use of marijuana, which is the drug most often used among teenagers. However, use of amphetamines ("uppers"), methaqualone, and LSD has also dropped. The use of amphetamines seems to have gone up in the late 1970s, so it seems especially significant that it is now dropping so quickly.

The use of barbituates ("downers") is also falling fast. In 1975, 11 percent of high school students surveyed said they'd used a downer of some kind in the past year; by the mid-1980s, that figure was down by more than half, to only 5 percent. The use of tranquilizers had gone down as well.

Finally, the use of PCP, or angel dust, also seems to be dropping. The use of this drug peaked in 1979, and has been falling more or less steadily ever since.

In other words, the 1960s and 1970s saw many high school students reporting the frequent, almost daily, use of various drugs. However, the 1980s have seen far less interest in drugs, and those that are still getting high seem to be doing it less often. High school students are also reporting a drop in the length and intensity of their "highs," which may mean that "heavy" drug use is far less popular than it used to be.

Cocaine is one drug that peaked in the early 1980s, rather than the late 1970s. Because of its high price, cocaine used to be virtually unknown among young people. With its growing use in the sports and entertainment communities, this drug became more well-known, and is now found among professionals and executives in may industries. However, the widely publicized deaths of several sports and Hollywood figures who were killed by cocaine overdose helped to make this drug less popular. In the early 1980s, some 12 percent of all high school students said that they had tried cocaine sometime in the past year. By the mid-1980s, this figure had declined, but only very slightly. Now, with the increased availability of cocaine-derived drugs like crack, which make cheap forms of cocaine easily available, this drug and its derivatives may be on the increase again. Experts are concerned about this trend, since the medical side effects of cocaine and crack are far more dangerous than those of marijuana.

Even though it seems that drug use among teenagers is declining, American teens probably use more illegal drugs than young people anywhere else in the industrial world. Almost two-thirds of U.S. teens have tried some kind of illegal drug before they leave high school, and fully 40 percent have used some kind of illegal drug other than marijuana. At least one in every 18 high school seniors smokes marijuana every day, and almost one-fifth of all seniors have smoked marijuana daily for at least a month at some time in their lives. In addition, although daily tobacco smoking has declined since the 1970s, almost one-fifth of all high school students still smoke at least one cigarette a day, and about 13 percent of high-schoolers smoke more than half a pack a day. Some 30 percent of the high school students surveyed had smoked cigarettes sometime in the past month, and over one-fifth of these smokers were daily smokers.

Even though it's technically illegal for most teens to drink, for many years, alcohol was considered better for teenagers than other kinds of drugs. Partly because adults had a drinking culture of their own, they found it easier to deal with a teen who got drunk than with a kid getting high on marijuana or tripping on LSD. Far more government money and attention has gone to the "drug problem" than to the "alcohol problem," and media attention is more often focused on teen drugs, than on teen drinking.

Yet drinking among teenagers may be a far more serious problem than drug use. Far more teens drink than do drugs—almost 93 percent of the high school seniors in one survey said they had used alcohol, with over two-thirds of all seniors saying that they had used it within the past month. And the health problems related to alcohol are very serious. One study showed that many junior high school students may smoke marijuana on a daily basis—but that their "smoking" consisted only of sharing a puff or two off the same joint with very little physical effect. These same students may go on drinking binges once every month or so, an activity that, over the long run, is far more dangerous to their health and safety.

Teens seem to be starting to drink at earlier ages than before. Over half of the seniors in one survey said they had started drinking before they started high school. This was a far higher figure than for teens surveyed in the mid- to late 1970s. About 10 percent of these seniors said they'd started drinking in the sixth grade; over 22 percent said they'd started in the seventh or eighth grade; and over 23 percent said they'd started in the ninth grade.

Heavy drinking went up sharply in the late 1970s. It seems to have started to drop slightly, but is still high enough to disturb many experts, who are concerned about the long-term health effects of heavy drinking on teenagers. Heavy or "party" drinking was defined as having had five or more drinks in a row on at least one occasion sometime in the past two weeks. The highest rate of this heavy drinking was in the late 1970s, when 41 percent of all seniors surveyed said they'd been drinking that heavily. By the mid-1980s, the rate was down, but only slightly, to 39 percent. It isn't clear whether teens who would have been taking drugs in the 1970s are turning to alcohol in the 1980s. But it *is* clear that almost every single high school student in the country has to deal with the heavy and regular drinking of friends and classmates. Nearly one-third of the seniors surveyed said that all or most of their friends get drunk at least once a week.

When teenagers are surveyed about why they like to drink, they often don't give any specific reason. Most just say they like the way it feels, or that it's a nice way to spend an evening with friends. Many teens feel pressure from their friends to drink. The pressure isn't direct—no one comes right out and says, "You aren't cool if you don't drink." But you may feel indirect pressure, the fear of being so different from all of your friends that you'll be left out if you don't drink when they do. Some teens "fake out" their friends—take a glass or a can of liquor, find a way to empty it somewhere, and then pretend to be drunk—just so they won't feel like the only one who doesn't want to drink.

Most teenagers don't see much risk in drinking. A survey of high school seniors found that only 23 percent thought that much harm could be caused by having one or two drinks every day. Only 25 percent thought there was any great risk involved in having five or more drinks once or twice each weekend. Although over two-thirds of these seniors thought that a person was taking a great risk if he or she took four or five drinks a day, almost one-third of the students didn't even see that much drinking as a risk.

In fact, there is a whole range of risks associated with heavy and regular drinking, from dried-out, blotchy skin to severe stomach and liver problems to the danger of dying or killing someone in a car accident. It's interesting that the 1980s have seen some increases in teens' perceptions of drinking as a risk. Perhaps because adults are also becoming more health-conscious, the percent of seniors who said that occasional heavy drinking was a risk rose from 35 percent in the late 1970s to 42 percent in the mid-1980s. About 3 percent of this 7 percent change took place in a single year—the same year in which seniors also reported fewer of these binges than ever before. It seems that when teens think something is dangerous, they're less likely to do it.

Likewise, in the late 1970s, students seemed to go easier on weekend party drinking. By the end of the decade more students were saying that such drinking was probably all right. But in the 1980s, students started changing their minds. By the mid-1980s, more and more teens began to disapprove of such drinking, until almost 60 percent said that they didn't think it was a good idea.

About half the seniors surveyed thought that their friends would disapprove of heavy drinking on weekends. Even more—74 percent—thought their friends would disapprove of them taking one or two drinks a day. Still more—86 percent—said their friends would strongly disapprove if they were drinking heavily every day.

So the statistics on teen attitudes actually show a contradictory situation. On the one hand, teens' own attitudes about heavy drinking are fairly tolerant. They don't see much risk in it—and many of them report that they are heavy drinkers themselves. On the other hand, teens think that their friends would disapprove of heavy drinking. Maybe this confusion comes from the mixed messages in the adult world. If adults tell you not to drink, but drink themselves, or if school tells you how dangerous drinking is while liquor ads, TV shows, and movies tell you that drinking is fun and glamorous, it's hard to know what to think. In the end, the only way to decide is to learn all you can about the contradictory messages, and about the effects of different kinds of drinking. You can't really think clearly about drinking until you think about the way it fits into your whole life—the way you spend time with friends, the way

you handle your problems, the way you feel about yourself.
(There will be more information on drinking and how it might
affect you in chapter 3.)

Just as with drinking, many teens feel pressure from their
friends about taking drugs. Again, the pressure is usually not
direct. No one threatens to leave you out of the next party if you
don't get high at this one. But it's very difficult to be in a situation where everyone else seems to be having fun doing something that you don't want to do.

The pressure to try drugs comes very early these days. One
survey found that close to 58 percent of the 300 third- to
seventh-graders surveyed said that they were under "a lot" of
pressure to smoke marijuana. Another survey of teenagers
found that about half felt pressured to try marijuana by the time
they were in seventh grade.

Parents may not seem to be much help in dealing with these
pressures. Although 58 percent of the elementary and middle
school students reported "a lot" of pressure to try marijuana,
only 4 percent of these kids' mothers thought their children
were under pressure. The teen years are already a time of conflict between parents and kids. The issue of drugs may make
that conflict even more intense.

Some parents, of course, are sensitive to how difficult these
issues can be. They offer useful advice and practical ideas on
how to cope with decisions about drugs. But many teens feel
that their parents could never understand the pressures they're
up against—with drugs or with anything else. Teens often say
that even when they do try to explain something to their
parents, the parents don't listen, or try to pretend that things are
better than they are. Nevertheless, it's best to try and have an
ongoing dialogue with your parents on the subject. Believe it or
not, they may be able to help you think these issues through.

Sorting things out can be complicated, especially when your
friends' and classmates' attitudes may vary. In some schools,
those who do drugs are considered "the elite," people who are
too sophisticated to get high on plain old booze. In other
schools, the "druggies" are looked down upon as sleazy and
unsuccessful.

In an atmosphere where messages are so mixed, it's hard to make good decisions. If your parents or teachers are telling you that smoking one joint of marijuana is just as bad as taking one hit of crack, and that all drug use is categorically bad, how do you put that together with the movies and TV shows you see, where adults seem to do a whole variety of drugs with no problems whatsoever? If your own or your friends' experience shows that some of what adults are saying is incorrect, how do you know whether you can believe any of it?

In the end, the decisions you make are up to you. Simply rebelling against whatever you hear at home or in school isn't an expression of real independence. It's still being controlled by what adults are saying—only instead of doing something because they want you to, you're doing it because they don't want you to. It's hard to resist pressures from parents, teachers, and friends, and it's hard to know what the consequences of taking drugs will actually be. But since there's no way to avoid these hard decisions, at least you can try to make them based on the best information you can, from the strongest and most independent place inside yourself.

Remember the two steps of judgment described in chapter 1:

1. Look at *all* the facts. Keep in mind everything you know about drugs or alcohol and the way this issue affects you.
2. Look at *all* your feelings. Let yourself be aware of every feeling that you have in connection with drinking or taking drugs. Ask yourself if these are feelings you enjoy having and, if not, what you can do about them.

It's much easier to remember the good parts of an experience than the parts that are not so pleasant. If we have done something that makes us feel ashamed, or angry, or frightened, it may seem easier just to "forget" what we have done or felt than to try to deal with it. The problem is, if you don't look clearly at the situation and your feelings, you are *never* going to be able to change them.

For example, if you say that you like to drink at parties because otherwise you feel shy, you are remembering the good parts of drinking—the times when your shy feelings seemed to go away and be replaced by better feelings. But what if you also feel ashamed and upset after drinking because you can't quite remember everything you've done, or because you know you acted foolishly and some people were laughing at you? It may seem easier just to pretend that didn't happen. That way, you have "forgotten" that there are any problems connected with drinking, and you can continue to drink.

But what about the problem you started with, the problem of feeling shy? By drinking to get over this problem, and then "forgetting" about the ways drinking didn't work (you still feel shy before the next party and you have to get drunk again; you feel shyer than ever when you remember the silly things you did), you've giving up any chance of really solving the problem. You'll keep trying a solution—drinking—that really doesn't work. You're not giving yourself the chance to find out that it doesn't work, because you're pretending that it does. Would you rather pretend to solve your problem, or really solve it?

You may be perfectly comfortable with your relationship to drinking and drugs, whatever that relationship is. If so, you have nothing to be afraid of in looking very closely at every part of your experiences and your feelings. If everything is really all right, the closer you look, the better you'll feel. If you find that the idea of thinking about your relationship to this issue is making you very uncomfortable, that's probably a sign that there is something that is not working for you. Have the courage to keep looking, to find out what is bothering you and how drinking or taking drugs relates to it. Only by looking at your experience and your feelings can you decide what decisions *you* really want to make.

3

Hard Facts About Drinking

Of all the mixed messages our society gives out about mind-active drugs, the messages that are the most mixed are probably those about alcohol. Alcohol hasn't been illegal for adults in this country in over 50 years—but in most states, alcohol is illegal for all teenagers, or for those under the age of 18. Movies, television commercials, and advertisements make it look as though drinking were a normal part of a "sophisticated," adult life—but high school drug-education classes tell you that drinking is bad for your physical and mental health. It probably won't surprise you that even the experts disagree about issues like how much social drinking can be harmful, or what the difference is between regular "social" drinking and a serious addiction to alcohol.

What this chapter will try to show you is that there are no simple answers to the question of how drinking will affect you—but there are some answers. Every person is affected differently by alcohol. Some people can drink an enormous amount without seeming to be affected by it. Others are affected by half a can of beer. Some people's livers are extremely sensitive, so that after years of "moderate" drinking, they discover that they've developed cirrhosis of the liver and protest, "But I've never even been drunk." Some people quickly develop a dependence on alcohol almost from the moment of their first drink; other people may drink "casually" for months or years, then wake up one day to realize they've become highly dependent on alcohol.

Variations exist not only between people, but over the course of one person's life. Whether you've had anything to eat, how tired you are, or what your mood is may well affect your susceptibility to alcohol. And no matter how well you handle liquor at other times, drinking is highly dangerous to anyone who is planning to drive, and to anyone who is pregnant.

Because drinking is such a big part of our culture, and because there are no easy answers where alcohol is concerned, it's especially important for you to take responsibility for the choices that are right for *you*. This chapter will provide information that will be helpful as you try to decide what place alcohol has in your life, and what place you want it to have.

The Physical Effects of Drinking

Let's start by looking at the physical effects of drinking. There are 100 or 150 calories in every glass of wine, beer, or liquor. That's about as many calories as you'd get in two pieces of bread, one big spoonful of mayonnaise, or over 100 slices of cucumber. Alcohol operates like a food, but with a very high sugar content. People who are especially sensitive to sugar, such as people with diabetes, are warned to be very careful about drinking or to avoid alcohol altogether.

If you have gone for six hours without eating, your body has run out of the energy that it stores in your blood sugar. Your body then needs to make more energy (unless you eat something). But alcohol inhibits this process. That's why drinking on an empty stomach can make you so tired so quickly. The alcohol in the drink keeps your body from making energy. Alcohol also makes it more difficult for your body to process vitamins and calcium. People who have drunk heavily or regularly for years are sometimes found to be suffering from malnutrition. This is because of the way that alcohol keeps the body from absorbing nutrients.

What happens when you take a drink? Alcohol starts in the mouth and throat, of course. In fact, about 20 percent of the alcohol you drink is absorbed int the body directly through the mouth and throat. Alcohol goes from the throat down through your esophagus—the tube that connects the mouth and throat with the stomach. It then goes into the stomach, from where it is absorbed by the intestines. Eventually, it travels into the liver. The presence of alcohol in these parts of your body has short- and long-term effects. These affects, as we've said, are different for different people. And even for the same person, these effects may vary, depending on the person's diet, emotional state, and general fitness. The more research that is done, however, the more scientists are tending to find that even "moderate" levels of drinking—two drinks a day at most—have long-term medical consequences.

Here are some of the possible effects alcohol can have on the different parts of your body as it travels through your system:

Mouth & Throat	Over long periods of time, heavy drinking can result in *cancer of the mouth and throat*, especially if the heavy drinker is also a heavy smoker.
Stomach	Alcohol slows down the process of the stomach emptying its contents into the intestines. It also increases your stomach's production of acid. Stomach problems are common among heavy drinkers, especially *gastritis* (an inflammation of the stomach walls), and *ulcers* (raw sores in the stomach walls).
Intestines	The intestines are supposed to absorb nutrients from the food we eat. Since alcohol interferes with this process, *diarrhea* can result.

Liver

The liver can handle only so much alcohol at one time. This amount varies in different persons, and in the same person at different times. An overloaded liver can suffer from three types of damage:

1. *fatty liver.* The body "burns" fat to produce energy. But if liquor is available to "burn" for energy instead, the normal amount of fat is not burned. This extra fat accumulates in the liver.
2. *alcoholic hepatitis.* This is an inflammation of the liver.
3. *cirrhosis.* The combination of alcohol and poor nutrition leads to scarring of the liver tissue. So much of the liver is scarred that the liver can't do its work of processing and cleaning the blood. There seems to be some relationship between the cirrhosis caused by alcohol and cancer of the liver.

Pancreas

The pancreas produces insulin, which helps the body process sugar. It also produces an enzyme that helps the body digest food. Heavy drinking can lead to *pancreatitis* (an inflamed pancreas), and to *pancreatic insufficiency* (a pancreas that doesn't function properly). Again, there may be some link between alcohol and cancer of the pancreas.

Heart

Moderate drinking—two to four drinks a day—can increase the heart rate and raise blood pressure slightly. Heavy drinking can *raise blood pressure* much more. Interestingly, although heavy drinking seems clearly bad for the heart, there is some evidence that moderate drinking may help prevent heart attacks, possibly because it helps some people relax.

Most of the effects we've discussed are the long-term effects of prolonged heavy drinking. They are important to know about because often a drinker will not be aware of these risks until it's too late. There is no way to notice the possibility of cirrhosis of the liver without regular medical checkups, and once you've got it, there is no cure. Because people's sensitivity varies, someone who doesn't consider himself or herself a heavy drinker may discover that drinking has in fact led to cirrhosis. The affected person's liver may have been more sensitive to alcohol than his or her brain was. That's why people notified of their cirrhosis may say, "But I was never even drunk—I only had a drink or two at parties!" Likewise, conditions like ulcers and high blood pressure can develop over long periods of time. Once you have developed these conditions, you can combat them, but you cannot ever get rid of the possibility that they may recur.

However, there are other consequences of drinking that happen in the short-term, are noticeable, and are caused by only "moderate" drinking. If you drink, you may have noticed some of these conditions, but not realized that they were related to your drinking:

Upset stomach. We've already seen how heavy drinking can cause severe gastritis by inflaming the lining of your stomach and increasing the production of acid. But even one night of drinking can make you feel queasy the next day for a mild attack of gastritis.

Diarrhea. If you have a few beers at a party and you wake up the next day with diarrhea, you might think it was something you ate. But it was more likely something you drank. Since alcohol interferes with the small intestine's ability to absorb food, water floods the large intestine to get rid of the unused food. In the long run, that can lead to malnutrition—because your body isn't using the food that you're eating. But in the short run, you may face a bout of diarrhea.

Anemia. If you've been drinking a lot lately and you notice you're feeling "blah," it might just be too much partying. But it might be a form of anemia, or not enough red blood cells. Alcohol is poisonous to the bone marrow cells that make red blood cells. Not enough red blood cells will leave you feeling weak and easily tired out. Even if you're taking iron and vitamin B supplements, it may not help—alcohol interferes with your body's ability to use those vitamins.

Skin problems. Alcohol can interfere with your sleep patterns. Besides tiring you out, this is bad for your skin. While you sleep, your skin sheds the day's dead cells. If you don't get enough resting time, the shedding process may not be completed. Alcohol also opens up your blood vessels, making your face feel warm and look red or blotchy. If you've got acne, alcohol can make it worse. If you have a tendency to oily skin, a drink can increase your skin's production of oil. Finally, alcohol is a diuretic—it helps your body get rid of water. That means that alcohol can dry your skin out at the same time that it's making your skin more oily, blotchy, and red.

Decreased fitness. Because alcohol is a diuretic—something that helps to rid your body of water—it can lead to the headaches that people associate with hangovers. Your brain needs a certain amount of fluid in it. When alcohol reduces the level of this fluid, it feels as though something was pulling your brain down—that awful feeling of a hangover. This lack of fluid also affects your perception and coordination. That's why athletes aren't supposed to drink the night before a big game or a big race. Over the long term, alcohol weakens your muscle fiber and irritates your joints, making sports—especially running—more difficult and dangerous. This is true of even moderate drinking, if you continue to drink regularly and often. Finally, since alcohol intereferes with your body's ability to absorb calcium, drinking can weaken your bones. This is especially likely for women, who need more calcium as they get older.

There is a physical explanation for the effect alcohol has on you. It dissolves the fat of your nerve cells, increasing the liquids in those cells, making them temporarily inactive, and putting some of your brain cells out of commission. But most people don't think about drinking as just physical effect. It's also a mental, emotional, and social process. Drinking is something that you do with friends under certain circumstances, such as parties or celebrations. Or it's something that makes you feel high and excited—or something that makes you feel calm and relaxed. Some people say they "think better" when they've had a few drinks. Other people say they're more fun to be with. And since alcohol affects different people different ways at different times, the line between the physical effects and the social or emotional effects starts to blur. Just what does drinking really do to your mind and your emotions?

Several experiments with alcohol offer some interesting answers to that question. In one experiment, people were given club soda and told that there was vodka in it. Many of them began to act as though they had been drinking—loosening up, becoming more aggressive, even walking unsteadily. In a related experiment, people were given alcoholic beverages and told that they were only being given soda. Many of these people did not show signs of drunkenness. One man who was especially worried about his drinking, but who felt he needed several beers each evening to relax, went with his psychiatrist to an experimental room in a university psychology department. The psychiatrist told the man he was pouring him a few "beers," which in fact were only "near-beer," a nonalcoholic drink that tastes like beer. The man became quite relieved in the midst of his second drink and began to describe the wonderful feeling of relaxation that he always started to get halfway through the second beer. When the psychiatrist revealed that the man had been drinking near-beer, the man was astonished. "Do you mean I've been making *myself* relax?" he asked.

Studies suggest that in different cultures, people respond to alcohol in different ways. In many parts of the United States, it is acceptable for drunken men to become more aggressive, louder, and more physical—so many men react in just that way.

In other cultures, a person who has drunk a good deal is expected to fall asleep—and many drinkers do indeed fall asleep. The experiments with the "real" and "false" drinks show that, sometimes, what you think you're going to do when you're drunk, or what your friends expect, can be even more important than the liquor itself.

There's no doubt that the physical side of drinking plays its part in how alcohol affects you. Most researchers agree that heavy drinkers may undergo "withdrawal" if they stop drinking. These drinkers' bodies have become so used to the neurochemical reaction that alcohol produces that their bodies have great difficulty in functioning without the help of alcohol. These "heavy" drinkers must usually be drinking six or more glasses of liquor—or beer, or wine—a day before physical withdrawal becomes a problem.

But what about people who drink less than that? Are they completely safe from dependence on alcohol?

No, because dependence on alcohol is more than a physical process. As the experiments with the "real" and "false" drinks showed, people use alcohol to achieve certain effects that they find pleasant or necessary. People who can't loosen up at a party or with a date until they've had a few drinks may be highly dependent on alcohol—even if they haven't got an actual physical addiction.

Some researchers talk about three different types of dependence on alcohol. There is *physical dependence*, when the body needs the neurochemical reaction produced by alcohol in order to keep functioning. Then there is *psychological dependence*, when people feel that they need to drink in order to be able to do something—face a difficult situation, loosen up sexually, enjoy a party, unwind at the end of a day. Finally, there is *social dependence*, when a social situation like a party or celebration makes you feel that you have to drink more than you really want to. All of these forms of dependence are ways of using alcohol to accomplish something that you feel you can't do on your own. In a way, they mean that you've lost the *power of choice*. If you are dependent upon alcohol in one of the ways listed above, it means that you no longer feel you have the choice of whether or not to drink. In some or many or even all situations, you feel that you *must* drink.

Many people have ways to get around facing their own dependence on alcohol. They decide that certain kinds of drinks don't "count." Beer may not be seen as the same as whiskey, for example. Or a glass of wine with dinner might not seem like drinking. But the fact is, from your body's point of view, all forms of alcohol are, if not the same, then very close. Your body reacts differently to beer, wine, and liquor. it probably has the most difficult time digesting hard liquor, especially if the liquor is straight. But is is true that there is the same amount of alcohol in a 12-ounce can of beer, a five-ounce glass of wine, or a 1 1/4-ounce shot of liquor.

Other people think that it "doesn't count," if they only drink at parties, if they never drink alone, or if they always have the same number of drinks. And in fact, these people may not have any dependence on alcohol. But, on the other hand, they might. The only way to tell whether or not you are dependent on alcohol is to give it up for a while and see what happens. Do you feel a strong sense of loss? Do you become very anxious and frightened? Do you find yourself counting the days—or the hours—until you can start drinking again? If not drinking—or the idea of not drinking—makes you very uncomfortable, you may need to get help in coping with your drinking. Even if you don't have an actual addiction to alcohol, you may have developed a dependence on it. Seeing a counselor or working with a support group like Alcoholics Anonymous or Alateen may help you feel that you've regained your power to choose.

No matter what other decisions you make for yourself about drinking, there is one time when nobody should drink—before getting into the driver's seat of a car. The number-one killer of teenagers in the United States is not cancer or heart disease or any of the other long-term sicknesses that kill most adults. The number-one killer of U.S. teenagers is accidents that are related to drunk driving.

Because your body develops a tolerance for alcohol, a regular drinker tends to need more and more alcohol to feel the "buzz" that makes you feel high. Thus a regular drinker may not feel "drunk," even after a few drinks. How you feel, though, has very little to do with how fast your reflexes are or how good your depth perception is. Someone who has been drinking will probably feel like he or she is more able to drive than is actually the case. If you have had even one drink within the past hour, you do not have the reflexes, perception, or judgment to drive, no matter how competent or powerful you may feel about other things.

Another time that no one should drink is during pregnancy. Think about what it feels like when you take a drink—how it affects your head, your stomach, your heartbeat. Then think about how this same drink would affect a tiny baby, weighing only a small percentage of what you weigh. If a pregnant woman drinks, so does the fetus—and the effects of alcohol on a growing fetus are much more severe than on a fully-grown adult. Babies whose mothers drank regularly during pregnancy can be born with Fetal Alcohol Syndrome—a ready-made addiction to alcohol. And if you can imagine the pain and difficulty of an adult who tries to withdraw from a physical addiction to alcohol, you can imagine how much more painful and dangerous this would be for a newborn.

Whether or not you want to drink, how much, and in what circumstances, are questions that you will be facing throughout your whole life. The answers to these questions will be different for everybody. Some people may discover that they don't like alcohol at all. Or they may consider that drinking is morally wrong. Or they may discover that their allergy or potential dependence on alcohol is so great that even one drink is too many.

Other people may decide that they enjoy drinking, and that they can find comfortable ways to make drinking a part of their lives. They will know how to tell the difference between drinking that is enjoyable and drinking that is the only way they know how to have fun; drinking that helps them unwind once in a while and drinking that is absolutely necessary for their well-being. They will understand that there are situations in which drinking is inappropriate or dangerous—such as before driving or during pregnancy. They will also know how to monitor their own drinking, to discover if they are using alcohol in a way that covers up other problems or feelings that might be better faced head-on.

Whatever you decide about drinking, remember that it is your power of choice that is the most important. You want to make decisions that increase your control over your life, rather than take that control away. More information on choices, addictions, and how to say "no" will be found in chapter 5 of this book.

4

Hard Facts About Drugs

In this society, many drugs are available to you. Some are legal; some are legal for adults only; some are legal under certain conditions—such as with a prescription; and some are completely illegal. All of these drugs—caffeine, nicotine, diet pills, amphetamines, crack, marijuana, alcohol, heroin, cocaine, LSD, PCP, and the rest—have a wide variety of effects on a wide variety of people. All of the drugs named can be addictive under some circumstances. Many of the drugs named above are highly addictive under *all* circumstances. Some people seem to have a tendency to become quickly addicted to some drugs while remaining relatively immune to the effects of others. Some drugs seem to cause dependency in just about anybody, no matter how well the person is able to handle other types of drugs.

If this seems confusing, that's no surprise. It *is* confusing. From the time that you're old enough to have access to any of the drugs listed above, you're hit with a mass of confusing information about them. The actual physical consequences *for you*, and the social and emotional consequences *for you*, get lost in the cross fire. Your parents and teachers may tell you that all drugs are bad. Your friends may tell you that they've never had any problems smoking pot, or doing coke, or taking speed.

One day you might read an ad in a national magazine telling you how taking diet pills can change your life. The next day in health class you read an article that explains how the caffeine in ordinary coffee and tea is bad for your heart, your blood pressure, and your sleep patterns. Adding to the confusion is your own commonsense observation and experience. Perhaps you've seen how one or two cups of coffee don't do anything for your mother, while even half a cup makes your father so nervous he can't sleep all night. You may know one friend who seems to have a truly amazing capacity for pills or pot or booze, and another friend who's gotten really messed up on small amounts of those substances.

What accounts for this bewildering variety? It's simple: people are different. Our emotional states, our anatomies, our social lives, our diets, and a hundred other factors all affect how we respond to different drugs. And these factors vary for every one of us, especially during adolescence. Hormonal and emotional changes can make it very difficult to tell the source of a physical or emotional reaction.

Yet it's also true that decisions about drugs are important decisions, some of the most important decisions you will have to make as a teenager. You may have to live for years with the results of those decisions. Some drugs, like heroin and crack, are highly addictive—almost no one can use them even a few times without developing a strong dependence that includes severe physical reactions to any decrease in the amount of the drug. Other drugs, like marijuana, alcohol, and cocaine, may have long-term physical effects that you don't notice right away, but which will continue to affect your emotional growth and your mental and physical well-being. Using any kind of drug, whether legal or illegal, always has social and emotional consequences—that is, you may find that taking diet pills or smoking pot changes how you feel, how you act, how you spend time with friends, how you handle family problems.

Of course, one way to avoid the problems that drugs can cause is simply to decide never to take any of them. But many teenagers are tempted at least to think about the question a little longer before making such a decision. The information in this chapter should help you sort out the various consequences you may expect to fact regarding different types of drugs, primarily the illegal ones. Some consequences are easy to see. Others are hidden, or only show up after a few years. Some consequences may apply to everybody; others to only a few people. When you think about decisions that have to do with drugs, be sure that you are being honest with yourself about the consequences that come with your choices. Remember the ways in which you are like other people, and not like other people, so that you can keep making the decisions that are right for you.

Effects of Drug Intake on the Body

A drug affects your body in five steps: (1) absorption, (2) distribution, (3) action, (4) metabolization, and (5) excretion. These steps may take place in a slightly different order for some drugs, but all five usually happen for most drugs.

Absorption is the way the drug enters your body in the first place. Most drugs are swallowed, passing through the mouth and throat into the stomach. From the stomach, the drug passes into the intestine, where it is absorbed into the body through the intestinal wall. Alcohol passes into the body very quickly; amphetamines and other pills are absorbed more slowly. If a drug is smoked or inhaled, like marijuana, it crosses the lung's membranes into the bloodstream. A drug like heroin that is injected into the body is absorbed directly into the bloodstream. A drug like cocaine that is (usually) snorted is absorbed through the mucus membranes of the nose. The way a drug enters your body affects how quickly or slowly the drug will affect you. It also affects the parts of your body that are involved in the absorption.

Once a drug has been absorbed, it goes on to *distribution* throughout your body. Sometimes a drug is distributed to a part of the body where it is stored for a long period of time. This may mean that the drug continues to affect you. PCP is stored in the body and released over a long period of time; that's why it continues to affect people who take it for so many hours. Marijuana is stored in the body as well. Some researchers say they have found dangerous consequences from this long-term storage of marijuana, consequences that are not noticed while the person is smoking but that show up only after a few years.

A drug's *action* takes place when the drug combines with a specific part of a cell. This part is called the "receptor." The receptor has a normal function in your body that the drug disrupts. Sometimes this can be a good thing. If you are taking medication to make your failing heart beat more strongly, for example, the medication affects the "normal" functioning of your body in good ways. If your body is functioning in a healthy way, however, the drug's action will disrupt this functioning. These alterations can result in many side effects, no matter how good or bad the main effect of the drug or medication. For example, various drugs—whether legal or illegal—may cause loss of memory, loss of appetite, hallucinations, depression, or other mood changes.

Because your body's tendency is to fight against any type of disruption, it will try to neutralize any drug that enters it through *metabolization*. Some drugs are metabolized very slowly; others are metabolized quickly. Sometimes a drug is not even active in the form in which it is absorbed into the body, but becomes active after it is metabolized. Heroin is not active in its first form, but the body metabolizes it into morphine, which is active. How a drug is metabolized helps explain whether the effects of a drug last for a long or a short period of time. They also help explain just how hard a drug is on your body. Again, this process applies to all drugs, legal or illegal, prescribed by a doctor or taken for "recreation."

Finally, your body eliminates a drug through *excretion*. This process most often takes place after the drug has been metabolized into a form that can be excreted. Usually, drugs are filtered through the kidneys and pass out with a person's urine. You can see from this that your kidneys are affected by any drug you take. You can also see why urine testing is one way of performing drug tests.

Effects of Drug Intake

Step	Body Parts Affected	Possible Results
ABSORPTION— **HOW DRUG ENTERS** **BODY**		
swallowing	mouth, throat, stomach, intestine, bloodstream	gastritis (stomach upset)
smoking	mouth, throat, lungs, bloodstream	lung damage from smoke
snorting	mucus membranes, bloodstream	runny nose, ulcerated membranes
injection	skin, bloodstream	scarring, hepatitis, AIDS, other infection
DISTRIBUTION— **HOW DRUG PASSES** **THROUGHOUT BODY**	liver, bloodstream, ultimately, entire system	long-term storage of drug (e.g., PCP or marijuana); long-term strain on liver or other organs; impairment of memory or other mental function; emotional effects
ACTION— **HOW DRUG DISRUPTS** **THE NORMAL FUNC-** **TION OF A CELL**	heart	change in heart rate
	nervous system	slowed reflexes, loss of appetite, depression, emotional ups or downs
	brain	loss of memory

Step	Body Parts Affected	Possible Results
METABOLIZA-TION—BODY'S ATTEMPT TO "NEUTRALIZE" DRUG	varies	varies
EXCRETION—HOW DRUG LEAVES BODY	kidneys	kidney problems

Here are some of the most common categories of drugs and their usual physical effects. More detailed explanation and discussion follow the chart.

Type of Drug	Symptoms	Dangers
Marijuana (pot, grass, joint, reefer)	Altered perceptions, dilated pupils, lack of concentration and coordination, craving for sweets and increased appetite, laughter	Increased heart rate, impaired short-term memory, anxiety, lung damage, psychological dependence
Cocaine (coke, snow, nose candy, blow, toot)	Short-lived euphoria that changes to depression, nervousness, irritability; tightening of muscles; increased heart rate and possible irregular heart rate	Anxiety, shallow breathing, fever, tremors; possible death from convulsions, respiratory problems, or heart problems
Amphetamines (bennies, dexies, uppers, black beauties, pep pills, crank, speed, many diet pills)	Loss of appetite that often includes loss of weight; anxiety and disturbed sleep patterns; irritability; rapid speech; tremors; feeling of "high" or "power" followed by a crash	Disorientation, severe depression (from the crash), paranoia, increased blood pressure, fatigue. Can lead to malnutrition. In some cases, hallucinations.
Barbiturates, Sedatives, Tranquilizers (downers, ludes, 714s, yellow jackets, tranks, reds, blues, rainbows)	Intoxication, slurred speech, drowsiness, decreased alertness and muscle control	Rigidity and painful muscle contractions; emotional instability; possible overdose and death, especially when mixed with alcohol

Type of Drug	Symptoms	Dangers
Hallucinogens (acid, LSD, MDA, MCP, mescaline, peyote, psilocybin, STP, DMT)	Mood and perception changes; possible euphoria, paranoia, panic, anxiety, nausea, tremors	Unpredictable behavior, flashbacks, possible emotional instability and psychosis, possible genetic damage causing birth defects to future children
Heroin (H, smack, junk) *Morphine* (M, Miss Emma) *Dilaudid* (Little D) *Codeine* (School Boy)	Euphoria, insensitivity to pain, sedation, nausea, vomiting, itchiness, watery eyes, running nose	Lethargy, weight loss, hepatitis and AIDS (from shared infected needles), slow and shallow breathing, possible death when combined with barbituates

Common Categories of Drugs and Their Effects

The effects of marijuana can vary widely, depending both on the type of person using it and on the nature of the plant and the method of its preparation. Most drugs are affected by the individual's mood when the drug is taken; this is especially true of marijuana. Some people barely notice its effects; others experience hallucinations, body distortions, severe depression, or strong changes in perception.

The negative effects of marijuana include a loss of short-term memory and a reduction in the ability to learn. This is one reason why schools are so concerned about marijuana smoked during the school day. Some researchers claim that used over a long period of time, marijuana affects people's personalities, leading to a kind of emotional flatness and loss of interest in the world, as well as diminished will power and a lowered capacity to deal with frustration. There is also some evidence that marijuana, like other types of smoking, is bad for the lungs. Smoking marijuana may also have some impact on future children, possibly being related to birth defects.

One important fact about marijuana is the length of time it stays in the body. Since marijuana is stored in the fatty sections of body cells and in the fatty one-third of the brain, it takes a long time for this drug to be excreted from the body. The chemicals in one single joint take almost a month to clear from the body. If a person smokes more than one joint a month, the chemicals from marijuana are continually in the body, even though the person does not feel any "high" for more than a few hours after smoking.

Driving a car after having smoked marijuana is definitely as dangerous as driving while under the influence of alcohol. It only takes about one hour for the effects of one drink to wear off, but it takes up to five or six hours for the effects of a joint to wear off. Mixing pot and booze before driving is especially dangerous.

Nobody has talked about any physical symptoms of withdrawal from marijuana. This means that probably pot is not physically addictive. Some people talk about psychological addiction, however. This means that people who smoke pot regularly come to depend on marijuana's dreamy, relaxed feeling in order to deal with their lives. Even though there may not be any serious physical effects when a heavy smoker gives up marijuana, the person may be afraid to stop, or feel that stopping is just not possible.

Cocaine is a drug that has become far more well-known in the last few years. Formerly, most people who used cocaine "snorted," or inhaled it through their noses. Recently, a form of coke known as "crack" has become more widespread. Crack is smoked, or absorbed through the lungs. This use makes the effects of cocaine far more acute, and they are felt far more rapidly. It may take several minutes to feel the effects of snorting coke, and the "high" lasts for about 20 minutes to half an hour. Crack, on the other hand, is felt within a few seconds, and the short but very intense high lasts only for five or 10 minutes, followed by a very intense crash. Cocaine is psychologically and physically addictive to many people, but it usually takes from two to five years for the addiction to develop. Crack, because it operates so quickly, is also very quickly addictive. Almost without exception, users become addicted within the first few uses, sometimes from the very first use. That's because the high is so intense, and so is the crash, leading the user to want to take more crack immediately, in order to feel better.

Cocaine constricts the blood vessels. When cocaine is snorted, it can irritate the nose's mucus membranes, even causing ulcers inside the nose. Cocaine is more volatile than most other drugs. That means that people's reactions to it vary far more widely from use to use. A dose that was safe one day may speed the heart up to an impossible rate the next. Even athletes with exceptionally good hearts and good respiratory systems have been known to die from their first use of cocaine. Of course, many people continue to use cocaine for years. The problem for users is that there is really no way to know how you will be affected.

The physical effects of cocaine and crack are similar, except that crack's effects happen more quickly, and thus more intensely. The blood pressure goes up, the pupils dilate, and the heartbeat increases by one-third to one-half its normal speed. Using coke and crack can result in severe weight loss, insomnia, and psychosis.

It's interesting to notice the different effects that different patterns of use may have. One study done at the Yale University School of Medicine's department of psychiatry found that users who'd checked in for treatment were more likely to report mood disorders and psychiatric problems if they snorted coke. These users tended not to use very much cocaine each week—but instead they would go on "binges" where they used a huge amount of cocaine in a very short time. They tended to use cocaine to make themselves feel better, but in fact, only made their psychological problems worse. These people may not have had any psychological problems before they began snorting coke, but for some reason turned out to be especially sensitive either in body or mind to the effects of cocaine, creating a vicious circle for themselves.

On the other hand, while those who smoked cocaine seemed to have fewer psychological problems, they had far greater physical problems. The dangers of smoking cocaine in the form of crack or in other forms are far more severe than the problems of snorting coke. The possibilities for addiction are also far greater for people who smoke crack.

Amphetamines are used both as prescription drugs and as "street drugs." They're also sold over the counter as diet pills and various kinds of energy pills. Amphetamines, or "uppers," are the second most frequently used drug by high school students (marijuana is the first).

Speed, uppers, and diet pills have a quick and violent effect on the system. They soon produce an increased heartbeat, higher blood pressure, and often a feeling of anxiety or nervousness. Many people take amphetamines to lose weight, but this can result in medical problems like malnutrition and dehydration. People who try to stay physically fit, such as gymnasts and joggers, should be especially careful with amphetamines because of these drugs' bad effects on the heart. Someone who takes uppers regularly may find himself or herself in a constant state of nagging anxiety.

Barbiturates, sedatives, and tranquilizers are also sold by prescription and over the counter, as well as on the street. These "downers" are depressants, like alcohol, and can cause similar "drunken" symptoms: drowsiness, confusion, mood swings, poor coordination, and, in some people, agitation.

Downers are highly addictive. In recent years, as we have said, many women's groups have complained that doctors are far too free in prescribing such powerful tranquilizers as Valium to their women patients. These groups have noted that withdrawal from many tranquilizers can be more difficult and dangerous than heroin withdrawal and that the psychological consequences of taking these drugs regularly are very serious. If you are concerned that you or someone you know may be dependent on any form of tranquilizer, especially Valium, you should be aware that medical help is needed to get off these drugs. If a person withdraws from sedatives without supervision, he or she faces low blood pressure, convulsions, delirium, and even possibly death.

Often people who start out using uppers find themselves using downers to come down, and vice versa. The potential hazards associated with use of these drugs are sometimes overlooked because many of them are legal in some form and so don't seem to be as potent or dangerous as drugs that are illegal. It's important to remember that your body is affected by whatever you put into it, whether that substance is controlled or not. Everyone needs to be careful about how any kind of drug—legal, illegal, or in some gray area—affects the mind and body.

As we have seen, people take drugs for different reasons and respond to them in different ways. With both drugs and alcohol, people's tolerance varies widely, and so does the likelihood of addiction. With two drugs, however, heroin and crack, there is almost no margin of difference as far as addiction is concerned. These two types of drugs are different from all others in that they will almost certainly result in severe physical dependence for virtually anyone who uses them. Robert M. Stutman, New York's special agent for the federal Drug Enforcement Administration, recently commented about this difference. "What makes crack different from all other drugs," he said, "is the unbelievably quick potential for addiction . . . . Heretofore, the vast majority of teenagers who experimented didn't get into trouble with drugs." But, says Stutman, teenagers who smoke crack are beginning to change this pattern.

Neighborhoods where crack is sold are feeling the impact of quickly rising rates of violent crimes. Many community leaders are expressing concern about crack, which they feel endangers the young people of their neighborhood with its temptations as well as affects all people who are vulnerable to violent crime. Because cocaine was so expensive, it had been used primarily by upper-middle-class people, mainly white, who were better able to afford it. But crack's relatively low price and easy manufacture make it a problem for poor people as well.

Another form of drug use that is almost universally dangerous is mixing different drugs, or mixing drugs and alcohol. Drugs that a person may be able to handle in isolation become dangerous and unpredictable when mixed with alcohol or other drugs. Use of more than one drug at a time, or polydrug abuse, is frequently related to teen depression and suicide. It can produce long-term health problems far more severe than the use of drugs or alcohol by themselves, and may even produce brain seizures that leave the user unconscious. The unpredictable effect of combining drugs is something that even doctors prescribing substances for medical reasons must take into account. If even the experts can't be sure of how a patient will be affected by a drug combination, it's clearly best to leave that possibility alone.

The important thing to remember when thinking about drugs is to accept your own limits, to be honest about them, and to be aware of the real impact drugs can have on your life. Drugs produce powerful physical and psychological consequences that are all the stronger when we are troubled, under stress, depressed, or facing other problems in our lives. There is no way to judge the impact of drugs on you by their effect on someone else. You have no way of knowing how your diet, mental state, or metabolism compares to that of another person. That is why even doctors with years of practice and volumes of research still cannot always accurately predict the effect of a medication on any given person. That effect varies from person to person, and it varies for a particular person from day to day. If even doctors cannot predict how a well-researched, legal drug will affect a person's body, how much less can you predict based on someone else's experience how a drug will affect not only your body, but your mind and emotions. Never make decisions about drugs based on how they affect somebody else; you are not somebody else, you are you.

The teenage years are already times of difficult choices and radical changes. It's often hard to keep a clear perspective on what you want, what's possible for you, and how you feel about your life. Taking a chemical that affects your body and mind can make it all the harder to keep this perspective—and all the more necessary.

5

Making Choices

When thinking about addiction or dependence on drugs or alcohol, people often tend to approach the subject in black-and-white terms. "Either you have a problem or you don't," someone might say. "I can handle my drinking just fine, so I obviously don't have a problem." The popular images of the alcoholic as the Skid Row bum and the drug addict as the depraved street person feed the misconception that there is a clear line dividing "addicts" and "alkies" from "normal people."

Thinking of drug and alcohol dependence in terms of black and white has two effects. It tends to make people look down on those who have admitted their addictions or dependencies. And it tends to make "social drinkers" or "recreational drug users" very defensive about looking at their own use of chemical substances. If there are only two choices—addict or non-addict—the pressure to deny that you are in the "addict" category is enormous.

So perhaps a more helpful approach is to use the image of a spectrum. On one end of the spectrum, we have the people whose problems with chemical substances have become so severe that major parts of their daily lives have been interrupted, disrupted, or damaged. These peoples' alcohol or drug habits keep them from functioning adequately at school, at work, at home, in their friendships and love relationships, or in several of these areas. They may have severe medical problems resulting from their addictions. They may find themselves engaging in theft or prostitution to come up with the money to pay for their habits. This extreme fits the popular picture of the "addict" or "alcoholic."

At the other end of the spectrum, we could place those people who genuinely have almost no interest in drugs or alcohol. The people on this end of the spectrum may take an occasional drink or smoke marijuana occasionally, but if liquor and marijuana disappeared from the face of the earth tomorrow, these people might not even notice. Whether or not they occasionally smoke, drink, or use drugs, it's safe to say that drugs and alcohol have no real place in their lives.

Then, there are the people occupying the middle of the spectrum who have varying relationships to alcohol and drugs. They may have lives in which drugs or alcohol play a large part, particularly where certain events are concerned. For example, they may be unable to imagine a dinner party without wine or a Saturday night basketball game without beer. They may go for weeks without thinking about drugs or alcohol, but go on periodic binges on occasional weekends, emerging with a severe hangover or depression and the resolution to stay drug- or liquor-free for the next few months. They may find that sometimes they feel in control of their drinking or drug use, but that in times of extreme stress—exam week, a rough patch in a love relationship, a bad time at school or on the job—their drinking/drug use suddenly takes on a more compulsive quality. In other words, these people may not have a full-blown addiction that regularly disrupts their lives but they may have a dependence that affects the way they deal with their problems.

What's helpful about the "spectrum" approach to addiction and dependency is that it allows each person to focus on what he or she finds uncomfortable in his or her use of drugs or alcohol. It acknowledges that sometimes the very same behavior can have different meanings. One night the three beers you have at a party are just a way of having fun; the next night, they're something you've used to avoid dealing with your feelings about your friends, someone you love, or a decision you have to make. Approaching the problem in these terms takes some of the pressure off deciding whether or not you're an "addict" or an "alcoholic" while encouraging you to think about the role of drugs and alcohol in your life. Of course, your use of drugs or alcohol may indeed have gotten to the point where it is regularly affecting your life in unwanted ways. If so, you should think about getting help to deal with the situation. (See the appendix for some places you can get help.) But even if your use of drugs or alcohol affects your life only occasionally, or in minor ways, it's still worth thinking about. And you still may discover that you want help in learning other ways to cope with the problems that drugs or liquor may be covering up.

It's often difficult for people to admit that they need help coping with a problem. Our society places a great premium on independence and tends to look down on people who admit their weaknesses or problems. But the fact is everyone has insecurities or feelings of helplessness. Some people may seem to have it all together, but these people may be so frightened of admitting their problems that they have devised very good ways of hiding them, even from themselves.

Denial

Pretending that you don't have a problem when you really do is called *denial*. It means that you're denying a problem rather than really dealing with it. People practice denial for many reasons. They may believe that someone, for example, another family member, would be angry with them or look down on them if they admitted they had a problem. They may feel that admitting a problem would actually make the problem bigger, as though hiding a problem somehow makes it smaller or easier to manage. They may fear that they really can't deal with the problem, that the best they can do is pretend it doesn't exist.

The trouble with denial is that as long as you pretend you don't have a problem, you can't deal with it. Then the problem really gets out of hand. The problem—and your need to hide it—are controlling your life. For example, if someone felt that she had a problem drinking too much at parties but didn't want to admit it, she might feel out of control. First this person feels that she can't control her drinking, then she feels that she must try to control what other people think about her drinking. She might go to great lengths to convince her friends and family that she has no problem, that she is either not drinking at all or that she is handling her drinking just fine. Because this person can't admit that she has a problem, she can't ask for help—and she has to spend a lot of time and energy hiding the problem. She may even find herself avoiding her family, choosing different friends who drink as much as she does, dropping out of activities she enjoys but that bring her into contact with people who might question her drinking—all to hide the fact that she has a problem. Her problem, and her efforts to hide it, are dominating her whole life.f

Here are some of the kinds of things people say when they are denying that they have problems:

- "That may bother other people, but it doesn't bother me."
- "Don't worry about me—I'm strong enough to handle anything."
- "Everybody gets drunk (or gets sick, or gets high, or passes out, or blacks out, or can't remember what they did the next day, or gets hungover)—I'm no different from anybody else."
- "I used to like so-and-so, but now she (or he) doesn't understand me."
- "I used to think good grades (or sports or drama or music or some other activity) was important, but I've grown out of that now."
- "I'm just the kind of person who likes to have a good time."
- "I only drink (or do drugs) on weekends (or at parties, or after school, or with such-and-such a friend)."

Do these sentences sound familiar? Does it make you uncomfortable to read them? Of course, anyone might say any one of these sentences for any reason. But if you are feeling uncomfortable, it may be because you use these phrases to cover up something that makes you even more uncomfortable.

It takes great courage to admit a problem and to ask for help in dealing with it, but it is such courage that is rewarded in the end. As you read through this chapter, let yourself be in touch with whatever fears or discomforts come up. If you allow yourself to look at a problem you've avoided for a while, you may find that the problem is smaller than you feared. Or you may find great relief in the idea that you can finally face this problem and start to cope with it, rather than run away from it.

When Is Drinking a "Problem"?

Because drinking is so common in our society, it's often difficult to distinguish between "problem" and "social" drinking. The questionnaires that follow are designed to help you think about the way you use alcohol. There are no right and wrong answers to any of the questions. But if you find yourself answering yes to a question, stop a minute and think about it. Let yourself react honestly to the feelings that the question provokes. Are you exhibiting a type of behavior that you are happy with? Had you realized that this was what you were doing? Is it difficult for you to admit the part alcohol plays in your life? If you find yourself answering "yes" to several of these questions, you may decide that you have a problem with drinking. Even if this problem only surfaces at particular times—on weekends, at parties, when you're having trouble with some particular aspect of your life—it's still a problem. Alcohol may be covering up your feelings or keeping you from facing a situation head-on, even if you are still able to function in your daily life. Think, then, about whether you want to change your relationship with alcohol.

1. Do you find yourself getting really drunk a lot?
2. Does your personality change when you're drinking? Do you pick fights, come on very strong with people you're interested in, say outrageous things, or otherwise behave in a way that you wouldn't if you were sober?
3. Do you find yourself having all kinds of accidents?
4. Are people around you starting to express concern,

either with your drinking or with your general appearance, behavior, performance in school, etcetera?

5. Do you feel you need alcohol to go through with something difficult, like a date? Do you drink *in order* to have a good time, rather than as *part* of a good time?

6. Do you hide drinks? Do you plan ahead when and where you're going to *drink next*?

7. Do you feel guilty about drinking?

8. Are you unable to discuss your drinking with anyone?

9. Do you sometimes forget what you did during whole periods of time when you were drunk?

10. Do you think and talk about drinking often?

11. Do you drink now more than you used to?

12. Do you sometimes gulp drinks?

13. Do you often take a drink to help you relax? Do you feel that you *can't* relax without a drink, or that you usually can't?

14. Do you drink when you are alone?

15. Do you keep a bottle hidden somewhere—at home or at school—for a quick pick-me-up? Does the thought of not knowing where you could get a drink if you needed one make you feel panicky?

16. Do you ever start drinking without really thinking about it?

17. Do you drink in the mornings to relieve a hangover?

18. Have you ever been arrested for an alcohol-related charge?

19. Have you ever missed school or work because of drinking? Because of a hangover? Because of being wiped out after a wild party or a night of drinking with a friend?

20. Do you dislike this quiz because it hits too close to home?

If any of these questions makes you nervous, or if answering these questions has made you want to think more about your use of alcohol, you may want to read some of the material or contact some of the organizations listed in the appendix. Your school counselor, a private therapist, or a local organization may also offer help in thinking about this issue, as well as reassurance that you are not alone.

If you are still comfortable with the idea of drinking but want to think about ways to do so in a more healthy manner, you might want to take some of the following suggestions:

- Set your own limit, based on alcohol's effect on your personal health and fitness goals. If you're going to a party or dinner with friends, decide how much is too much ahead of time, and stick to your limit.
- Have something to eat. Even if you can't eat a whole meal, eat something—especially a protein and a fat. A glass of milk, a piece of cheese, or some bread and butter will help soften alcohol's effect on your system.
- Sip drinks, don't gulp them. This will help you stay aware of how much you are drinking, and will make it easier to drink less over the course of an evening.
- Dilute your drink. A mixed drink is easier on your system than a straight shot of liquor. Wine is easier still. And beer is probably the best choice for someone trying to cut down on drinking, because beer fills you up more quickly than other kinds of alcohol. (That doesn't mean you should cut back on one type of liquor by increasing your beer drinking, however!)
- Don't drink to elevate your mood—to relieve feelings of anxiety, pain, or depression. Since alcohol is a depressant, it tends to perpetuate your mood, and can actually make bad feelings worse.
- Don't drink to signals, such as every Friday night, every big date, just before you go to bed to help you sleep, etcetera. If you can't imagine not drinking on a social occasion try it and see what happens.
- One or fewer drinks per hour will help prevent hangovers. It's drinking a lot in a short time that makes hangovers worse. Alcohol dehydrates you and makes it difficult to absorb vitamins. (If you find yourself going through elaborate rituals to prevent a hangover, this might be a sign that you are drinking in a way that threatens to disrupt your life.)

- Sprees or binges, where you drink a lot in a short period, are worse for your health than drinking a little at a time, so stay aware of your drinking patterns.
- Of course, you should never drink and drive. And never ride in a car driven by someone who has been drinking. Decide at the beginning of the evening how you will handle transportation: by having one of the group stay sober, by chipping in for a taxi, by arranging for someone else who is sober to pick you up, by using public transportation, by spending the night at the place you drink.
- Don't match other people's drinking. Different people have different body weights, different sensitivities to liquor, different emotional reactions, and so on. Women have less efficient livers than men, and usually have lower body weights, so they should not try to match men's drinking.

Finally, having read this material or having already made your decision, you may want to work on your ability to say "no" to a drink. Whether this means cutting out alcohol completely, or just stopping at the point that feels right for you, you might want some ideas for how to refuse alcohol when it is offered to you. These phrases might be helpful:

- "No thanks, I'm driving."
- "No, thanks, I don't want to get into trouble with my parents (teachers, friends, grandparents, etcetera)."
- "No, thanks, if I drink I'll lose my privileges (such as the use of the car)."
- "No, thanks, I don't like the taste."
- "No, thanks, I don't drink."
- "No, thanks, it's just not me."
- "No, thanks, I've got to study later (or pick up a friend, or get up early, etcetera)."
- "No, thanks, I've got a big day tomorrow (or a big game, or some other important activity coming up)."

- "No, thanks, I want to keep a clear head."
- "No, thanks, I usually end up embarrassing myself."
- "No, thanks, drinking makes me tired."
- "No, thanks, I'm on a diet."
- "No, thanks, I'm in training."
- "No, thanks, what else have you got?"
- "No, thanks."

A Look at Drug Use

Many of the issues that are raised when making choices about drugs are the same as those that come when alcohol is considered. Sal Gambino,* a senior counselor at Daytop Village drug treatment facility in New York City, says that it's often difficult to say no to drugs, especially if they're part of your social scene. "It takes courage to say no to a 'friend' who's offering you crack," says Gambino. But, he points out, that courage may help you to reevaluate the relationships that are based on drugs. "What kind of a friend is that?"

The choices concerning drug use are somewhat different than those surrounding use of alcohol because of the different social roles ascribed to the two types of chemicals. Alcohol use is considered primarily recreational. While some people in our society disapprove of drinking for moral reasons and might consider any kind of alcohol use to be wrong, or at least questionable, in many circles, however, alcohol use is accepted—for adults.

Drugs on the other hand, are viewed differently. Some, like marijuana, cocaine, and crack, are illegal and their use is disapproved of far more strongly than that of alcohol. Others, like diet pills, tranquilizers, and painkillers, can be considered medical rather than recreational, and may be legal for people of all ages under certain circumstances, such as with a doctor's

---

*Mr. Gambino speaks from his personal experience and not as a spokesman for Daytop Village.

prescription, or when sold over the counter. Even these "legal" drugs, however, can be used in "recreational"—and potentially dangerous ways. Likewise, antihistamines, headache pills, and similar "safe" over-the-counter medication can be dangerous, even deadly, when mixed with alcohol or other drugs.

What do these different attitudes mean to you and your relationship to drugs and alcohol? Well, being aware of these attitudes can help make you more aware of your own. Perhaps you know someone who thinks that any kind of drinking—or any kind of fun at all—is wrong. Perhaps you don't agree with such a view. Being aware of that view and of your disagreement with it can help you decide exactly what you *do* think about drinking. Just because some people don't see the difference between having fun, taking one drink, and getting completely drunk doesn't mean that *you* should equate those three actions. Just because someone is against all three actions doesn't mean that you have to be *for* all three.

Likewise, with drugs, you may not want to go along with all the prevailing attitudes. Just because some doctors think it's all right to prescribe diet pills or tranquilizers for some people doesn't mean that you necessarily want to cope with losing weight or calming down that way yourself. And certainly you want to be aware of the difference of using legal drugs like antihistamines for the purposes they were designed for versus using them with alcohol or other drugs in order to get high. If you are going to make choices about drug use in your life, it's important that you know what those choices are and not deny what you are doing by pretending that you are just doing what is legal or medically acceptable.

Different drugs have given rise to different patterns of use. Here are a couple of questionnaires designed to help you think through your relationship to marijuana and cocaine. These questionnaires are meant to help you see the role of these drugs in your life more clearly. If the questions make you uncomfortable, or if they make you want to find out more, you can look at the appendix for further information on reading material, organizations, and counseling.

Questionnaire on Marijuana
(Adapted from quiz developed by Potsmokers Anonymous, a group designed to help people with a dependence on marijuana)

- Can you remember the last time you went to a movie straight?
- Do you need a nighttime "J" to fall asleep? To relax?
- Would you rather stay home and smoke alone than go out with friends?
- Would you and your friends rather stay home and smoke than go out and do something else straight?
- Do you buy eyedrops by the case?
- Can you remember what life was like before you started getting high?
- Do you have an easier time with your boyfriend or girlfriend when you are high? Do you think sexual activity is better when one or both of you are high?
- Do you make emergency trips to your local market for munchies?
- Do you wake up feeling tired?
- Do you think pot is better for you than alcohol?
- Do you remember the last time you turned down a joint when it was offered to you?
- Do you get high before meeting a group of your non-smoking friends?
- Do you get nervous when your supply runs low?
- Did you ever forget who you were talking to on the phone . . . in the middle of a conversation?
- Do you feel that you can stop smoking any time you want to, only you haven't wanted to in months?

Questionnaire on Cocaine
(Adapted from a quiz developed by Dr. Mark S. Gold, founder of the 800-Cocaine Hotline)

- Do you have to use larger doses of cocaine to get the high you once got from smaller doses?

- Do you have three or more of the following physical symptoms: sleep problems, nose bleeds, headaches, sinus problems, voice problems, difficulty swallowing, sexual performance problems, nausea or vomiting, trouble breathing or shortness of breath, constant sniffling or rubbing your nose, irregular heartbeats, epileptic seizures or convulsions?
- Do you have three or more of the following psychological symptoms: jitteryness, anxiety, depression, panic, irritability, suspiciousness, paranoia, problems concentrating, hallucinations, loss of interest in friends, hobbies, sports, and other noncocaine activities, memory problems, thoughts about suicide, compulsive, repetitious acts like combing the hair, straightening of clothes, or tapping the feet for no reason?
- Are you afraid that if you stop using cocaine, your work or your social life will suffer?
- Do you think about cocaine when you are doing something totally unrelated to it, like talking to a friend or attending a class in school?
- Do you need to take other drugs or alcohol to calm down after using cocaine?
- Are you reducing contact with your friends who don't use cocaine?
- When you stop using cocaine, do you get very depressed or crash heavily?
- Do people keep telling you you're different than you used to be, or that you've changed a lot?
- Since you started using cocaine, have you ever wondered whether you would be able to live without it?

If you find yourself wondering about the role of other drugs in your life—speed, tranquilizers, diet pills, sleeping pills—then there is probably something in your use of them that you are not comfortable with. If any of the questions on the marijuana or cocaine questionnaires triggers a feeling of discomfort or nervousness, that's a signal that you have some thinking to do about the way you are using that drug. Sometimes people aren't ready to make changes in their lives until something really drastic happens—an accident, a major confrontation with a loved one, a really frightening experience. But with the courage to face honestly what's going on in your life, you can make decisions for yourself even about smaller problems. The important question to ask yourself is not "Is my life out of control because of alcohol or drugs?" but rather, "Am I happy with the relationship I have to alcohol and drugs?" If these questionnaires make you uncomfortable, it's probably a sign that there is something that you are not happy about.

If you decide that you aren't happy with some part of your behavior, then what can you do about it?

Perhaps, as you read this chapter, you are realizing that you have been using drugs or alcohol to avoid facing other kinds of problems in your life. Drugs or alcohol may not seem nearly as difficult to deal with as this other problem. You may be thinking something like, "I don't really like drinking at parties all that much. I don't like those hangovers the day after, either. But I'm so shy! How would I ever talk to someone if I wasn't drinking?"

If this is your reaction, you are actually very lucky. It means that you are actually pretty much in touch with what is really bothering you, and that you are ready to do something to make your life better. You might begin by thinking very practically about the problem you have identified. Don't think about what a terrible person you are ("Why am I so shy?"), think about *how to solve the problem* ("What could I do to have a better time at parties?"). For example, if your problem is feeling uncomfortable at parties, can you make a deal with a friend to go to the party with you? Can you get a friend's help in introducing you to people, or getting a conversation going with you, so you don't feel so awkward? Imagine if someone else came to you for advice about your problem. Would you give the person a hard time just for having a problem? Or would you try to think of ways that the problem could be solved?

Facing a problem that you have been avoiding is often scary and uncomfortable. If you have been pretending for a long time that there is no problem, you may feel ashamed to admit that there is one. You may feel as though everyone has been watching you, or laughing at you, or getting mad at you because of this problem. Or you may feel that you get along all right now, but that people will laugh, or look down at you, or get mad if you admit—even to yourself—that there's something in your life that you can't handle.

In fact, you may be surprised to find that admitting a problem—even to yourself—will actually bring you closer to other people. You may find that some people knew about your problem all along (whether it be a problem with drugs or alcohol, or another difficult problem, like feeling shy). Perhaps these other people have been wanting to offer you help, advice, or simply friendship for awhile—but were afraid to do so because they felt *you* didn't want them to know what was going on. You may also find that you have been afraid to let other people become close friends in order to keep them from finding out about your problem. Once you are not hiding part of yourself, you can relax and let people get a little closer. Most people are so concerned with their own problems, they don't have time to be very upset about yours—especially if you are not encouraging them to be critical by acting as though you are ashamed.

If you feel that you have a problem that you can't solve by yourself, there are many different kinds of help available. For people whose main problem does not have to do with drugs or alcohol, some kind of therapy or counseling is often very helpful. A therapist or counselor will keep what you say completely confidential. (If you have any doubt about this, ask. A therapist should be completely honest with you about whether he or she will discuss you with anyone else.) A good therapist or counselor will not judge you. Rather, he or she will carefully examine your feelings and perhaps even encourage you to explore feelings that you may think are "bad" or "dirty." A good therapist will help you see that all of your feelings are important, and that you have more choices than you may have thought you had about how to deal with the things that bother you. Your school counselor may be able to counsel you, or to refer you to someone who can. If not, check the phone book for a Mental Health Hot Line, a County Social Services Department, or a State Social Services Department, or look in the *Yellow Pages* under "Mental Health Services." Even Hollywood movie stars need help with their problems from therapists—so why should you be ashamed to get help?

Finding Help

There are a variety of kinds of help available to people who specifically want to change their relationship to alcohol or drugs. Individual therapy, group therapy, counseling programs, drug hotlines, rehabilitation centers, outpatient clinics, support groups, and many organizations that offer different philosophies about drugs and alcohol and different approaches to treatment. It's important to know that help is available, because many teens report that when they try to talk to parents, or counselors, or even therapists about their drug use, they often run into a brick wall. Many adults don't want to deal with these problems—perhaps because of their own fears and discomfort around drugs and drink. But if you want help, you should get it. Don't let other people's bad attitudes keep you from doing something for yourself.

Drug counselor Sal Gambino says that a big part of most drug treatment has to do with getting past the user's facade to the real feelings of the person beneath. "An image doesn't feel—a person feels," says Gambino. He explains that drugs and alcohol are a way of maintaining a safe image, so that the person doesn't have to deal with scary or painful feelings that are overwhelming or out of control. That's why many programs like Daytop Village use group therapy—a group of people who have had problems with alcohol or drugs talk together with the help of an experienced counselor, who may also be a former user. In group therapy, people express their fears about issues like not living up to parents' expectations. Over time they come to realize how they really feel, and how they can deal with those feelings, rather than trying to cover them up. Members of the group slowly build up trust in one another as each realizes that he or she is not alone—everyone has troubling feelings and everyone must learn new ways of coping with them.

An approach that is related to the group therapy method but works somewhat differently is the support-group approach. People who are trying to change their relationship to drugs or alcohol talk to each other about their problems, but not necessarily with a trained counselor present. People in the support group agree to be available to one another when someone has trouble, so that if, say, a group member wakes up in the middle of the night wanting a drink, he or she can call a member of the support group for help.

Perhaps, as you read this chapter, you are uncomfortable with your relationship to drugs and alcohol but you are thinking, "I don't need help. I can change my drug use or drinking by myself." If you can, more power to you. You're entitled to feel very good about yourself and your ability to make sound choices in your life.

But be careful. Sometimes people set little "tests" for themselves to try to prove that they don't have a problem with drinking or drugs. They say, "I won't drink for three days," or "I won't get high at the next party—that will prove I don't have a problem." They pass their tests or perhaps find a "good reason" for not passing them—"Oh, Louie will be hurt if I don't take a drink at his birthday party. I'll wait till the next party to stop drinking." Then they go right back to the same behavior that was giving them trouble before. If you feel that you are giving something up as a test, or in order to prove something, think again. You may be giving yourself a signal that you really *do* need help. If you knew someone who was trying to walk on a broken leg to prove it wasn't broken, would you think that person was being strong—or just stubborn?

Another thing to watch out for is replacing one kind of difficulty with another. Sometimes this is not really a problem. People who are trying to quit smoking cigarettes typically expect that they will be eating more than usual or chewing a lot of gum. They need something to replace their addiction to nicotine. Probably it is better for their health in the long run to overeat slightly while they are giving up the nicotine. As long as overeating doesn't become a permanent way of coping, it may be a good temporary solution.

But if you find yourself giving up one kind of liquor only to switch to another (cutting back on hard liquor but drinking even more beer) or cutting back on drugs only to start drinking or cutting back on either drugs or alcohol only to start overeating or dieting excessively or doing something else that feels out of control, then you know you haven't really solved your problem. And, again, you are probably sending yourself a signal that you need help. If you are, do yourself a favor. Listen to yourself. Get the help you need. Everybody needs help sometime—why should you be different?

Sometimes it may seem to teenagers as though all of life's problems can be resolved once "something else" happens—"as soon as I move away from home," "as soon as I finish school," "as soon as I get married." Because adolescence is a time of change and transition, you may feel as though you've got one set of decisions to make and then your life will be settled. But in fact, as life goes on, the choices keep coming. Life is a process of making and remaking decisions, and what seems to work at one stage just seems to get in the way at another.

Decisions about drugs and alcohol are no different than other decisions you have to make in your life. If you are a recovering alcoholic or addict, you have to keep deciding not to return to your former patterns. If basically you are unconcerned about the way you drink or use drugs but notice some recurring problems, you can keep rethinking your behavior and making different decisions about what you feel comfortable with and how you want to handle it. Even if you are not interested in drugs or alcohol now, you may find that at some point a stressful situation or an unusual circumstance will present you with a new problem or a different choice that you will have to confront.

The thinking you do *now* about the kind of life you want—and whether drugs and alcohol have a place in it—will be helpful to you throughout your life. That's because you are going to be facing decisions about drugs and alcohol for the rest of your life. You are going to be at parties where people drink, or perhaps at parties where people do drugs. You may have a doctor who prescribes tranquilizers or diet pills for you, or for someone you care about. You may have a friend who has trouble with drinking or with drugs. Your own attitudes about these issues may change as you get older and have more experiences. But the more practice you get now in thinking and making choices for yourself, the more comfortable you will be making choices later. Making choices may always be somewhat difficult—but it does get easier with practice! Start practicing now.

6

Families with Problems

Even if you are perfectly comfortable with your own relationship to drugs or alcohol, addiction and dependence may cause problems in your life. If a member of your family, or someone close to you, has a problem with drugs or drinking, you may feel that you share that problem. The pain and frustration caused by a family member's or friend's addiction is often as severe as the pain caused by actually having an addiction yourself.

In recent years, there has been growing attention paid to the families of alcoholics or drug addicts, but people still have many misconceptions about these family members. Many people believe that a family that includes someone with an addiction is a "bad" family. They may believe that a "good" family would cure the addiction, or punish the addict so badly that the problem would somehow be solved. Or some people may believe that it is a family's duty to somehow "protect" an alcoholic or drug addict from the consequences of his or her dependence. If you have a parent, a brother, a sister, or some other relative with a drug or a drinking problem, you may come to think that you are somehow responsible for this for a variety of reasons.

For example, you may have been told that it is your fault that this family member drinks. "If you wouldn't upset your father so much, he'd be all right," someone may have told you. Or, "Kim is jealous of you, that's why she's having problems."

Or, you may have been told that something you do might help your relative or friend to stop drinking or taking drugs. "If you'd be more help at home, your mother might be able to get it together," may be a message that someone has given out, with or without words. Perhaps you've been told to keep a younger brother or sister away from a bad crowd, or to keep an eye on a parent and somehow stop him or her from taking a drink. Even without meaning to, someone may have given you the idea that stopping another person from drinking or taking drugs is your responsibility. Therefore, you may reason, if the person continues with his or her addiction, it must be your fault.

Even in a situation where no one is actually blaming you for the problem, you may be made to feel that you should help out more to compensate for the person with the problem. Someone may have made you feel that you shouldn't get angry when your father drinks because "he can't help it," or that you shouldn't mind having to do all the cooking because "your mother is having a hard time right now." You may have gotten the message that you shouldn't mind giving up all your personal time in order to "help" the other person. Your family may agree that someone else's problems are *always* more important than yours; you may feel that you have to go along with this idea or you're a "bad" or "selfish" person.

All of these messages may have led you to feel guilty. If you feel responsible for getting another person to stop drinking or stop taking drugs, and the other person keeps on with the addictive behavior, then you may blame yourself for doing something wrong. You may feel that "if only" you were a better person, you could make things easier for your family.

How the Problem Drinker/ Drug User Affects You

Recognizing the Problem

Sometimes it's easier to believe that you are responsible for a problem than to admit that there's nothing you can do about it. And, in fact, if a member of your family is drinking or using drugs in a destructive way, there really isn't very much you can do about. That person's addiction is his or her own problem.

Likewise, there isn't anything you can do to make things better for your family. *You* are not your family's problem. Every member of your family is responsible for him- and herself. There is really very little you can do to make your parents feel better about a brother or sister who is causing them pain. You can't protect your brothers or sisters by taking the place of a parent with a problem.

What you can definitely do something about, however, is to recognize how the problem is affecting *you*. You can figure out ways of coping with your own anger, frustration, pain, and love for the family member in ways that will be more satisfying for you, so that another's drinking or drug use is not controlling your life.

The National Institutes on Alcohol Abuse and Alcoholism, the federal agency that studies alcoholism, estimates that there are currently 28 million people with alcoholic parents living in the United States, 6 million of them under 18. In New York State alone, some 3,000 family members of addicts are involved in city and state treatment programs. This is just a very tiny portion of the total, however, since there are 37,000 addicts in recovery programs in New York, and several hundred thousand more not currently in treatment programs. Nar-Anon, a support group for family members of narcotics users, has about 300 groups that operate throughout the country, and is aware that many more people need to be reached.

What these figures should suggest is that if a member of your family is using drugs or alcohol in a destructive way, you are far from alone. There are many, many other people who have faced the problems you have, and there are many organizations that offer help. First, however, you need to decide whether you are in fact from a family that includes a problem drinker or drug user. Because many families try to deny that there is any problem, continually covering up for the family member and putting on a good face to the world, it is often difficult and confusing to identify your own feelings. Alateen, an organization for young people whose lives have been affected by someone else's drinking, has developed the following questionnaire to help teenagers decide whether they have a problem with a loved one's drinking.

1. Do you have a parent, close friend, or relative whose drinking upsets you?
2. Do you cover up your real feelings by pretending you don't care?
3. Does it seem like every holiday is spoiled because of drinking?
4. Do you tell lies to cover up for someone else's drinking or what's happening in your home?
5. Do you stay out of the house as much as possible because you hate it there?
6. Are you afraid to upset someone for fear it will set off a drinking bout?
7. Do you feel nobody really loves or cares what happens to you?
8. Are you afraid or embarrassed to bring your friends home?
9. Do you think the drinker's behavior is caused by you, other members of your family, friends, or rotten breaks in life?
10. Do you make threats such as, "If you don't stop drinking, fighting, etc., I'll run away?"
11. Do you make promises about behavior such as, "I'll get better school marks, go to church, or keep my room

clean" in exchange for a promise that the drinking and fighting stop?

12. Do you feel that if your mom or dad loved you, she or he would stop drinking?
13. Do you ever threaten or actually hurt yourself to scare your parents into saying "I'm sorry" or "I love you"?
14. Do you believe no one could possibly understand how you feel?
15. Do you have money problems because of someone else's drinking?
16. Are meal times frequently delayed because of the drinker?
17. Have you considered calling the police because of drinking behavior?
18. Have you refused dates out of fear and anxiety?
19. Do you think that if the drinker stopped drinking, your other problems would be solved?
20. Do you ever treat people (teachers, schoolmates, teammates, etcetera) unjustly because you are angry at someone else for drinking too much?

Patterns of Denial

When people are faced with something that is very painful and seems out of their control, they sometimes try to deny that the problem exists. As we've discussed, this behavior is known as *denial*. One form of denial is to contend that the problem isn't really a problem because it can be dealt with or isn't bothersome. Another is to fantasize about the way things could be if only the problem didn't exist. People in families with drinking or drug problems often feel that if only the family member responsible didn't drink or do drugs all their other problems would be solved. Then they feel angry and powerless because they can't solve their problems as long as this other person is acting so badly. Children of families where a parent, brother, or sister has a drug or alcohol problem often tend to take on roles that are based on denying or covering up the problem. The following are some stereotypes that are commonly found in the families of alcoholics or drug addicts:

The Perfect Child or "Superkid" This person may be the one that everyone else in the family turns to to help make things better. The parent who doesn't have a drinking or drug problem may expect this child to take the addicted parent's place, to be the "man in the family," or the "little mother." Or this child may wish so badly that he or she had a "good" family that it becomes necessary to perform brilliantly at school and in the community, winning all sorts of honors and awards to help keep up the fantasy that everything is really all right. These people may be real leaders, and they may have real accomplishments or achievements, but they are also very easily worried by anything that appears to be a failing on their part, and they are very anxious if they feel that anyone does not like or approve of them. They are often the oldest children in their families and may have been expected to take care of the younger children, especially during times of difficulty with a family member's drug taking or drinking. The person in this role may feel that everything always depends on him or her, and that making even one mistake could somehow be "fatal" to him or her or to others.

The Rebel, or "Bad Kid" This child may have had an older brother or sister who was a "superkid." Between superkid and the family member who had the "problem," the Rebel may have felt that he or she had no chance at winning any attention at all. With "superkid" around, the Rebel probably couldn't get attention by being good, so decided to get attention by being "bad" or acting out in some way. "Superkid" may have tried to win the approval of adults; "the Rebel," on the other hand, has lots of friends and may be part of a strong group that offers support that is missing in the family. The Rebel tends to talk back in school, and may feel compelled to break rules just to see what happens. Sometimes families with problem drinkers or drug users tend to blame the Rebel for all their problems: "If you wouldn't be such a mess, your father wouldn't get so upset and start drinking," or "If you would just set a better example, your sister wouldn't act so wild." The Rebel may secretly feel that he or she *is* to blame for the family's problems. The Rebel may also be very angry at having to take the blame for someone else's behavior, and at not being able to get any attention except when doing something "bad."

The Clown This child grew up constantly aware that something bad might happen any minute. So he or she learned how to distract other people from their pain, hoping that by being funny or cute or cuddly, it would be possible to make other people forget their problems and maybe make the house a happier place. The Clown may be the center of attention in class, at parties, or with friends. He or she may "act out," or may have other more acceptable ways of getting attention. But no matter how much attention the Clown gets, it doesn't really solve the underlying problem. This person tends to be frequently nervous and confused. The confusion comes from not quite knowing what's going on in the family, exactly how the problems start, or where they come from. The nervousness comes from the nagging fear that someday there may be a problem that the Clown will miss, or will catch too late, and then, without the Clown's clowning to make things all right, things really will explode. Because the Clown has learned to be very good at making other people laugh, his or her depression and fear may not be noticed. The Clown may have learned to hide these painful feelings even from him- or herself.

The Caretaker This child may be similar to Superkid in many ways, but his or her focus is less on winning achievements than on helping other people to feel better. This child probably has many friends and is liked by adults as well. The Caretaker has developed sensitivity and tact, and often knows how to care for others meticulously. What he or she is not as good at is taking care of him- or herself. Caretakers may feel that if they don't take care of others, they aren't worth very much. It may seem to them that they are responsible for helping others at all costs, so that their own feelings always come last. These people may feel that it is wrong to want things for themselves, to have angry or negative feelings about others, or to be unable or unwilling to help another person at all times.

The Passive Child, or the "Adjuster" This is the person who never causes any trouble, but who seems to get lost in the crowd. When this person was growing up, the family problems may have seemed so difficult that withdrawal was the only way to cope. "I won't cause any trouble, and if bad things happen, I just won't think about them. Then they won't bother me," the Adjuster may reason. "I won't let anything upset me. Whatever happens, I can always adjust." The price of adjustment, however, is the great distance between this person and other people. The Adjuster may feel that no one really knows him or her, and that if friends knew what he or she was "really" like, they wouldn't stay friends very long. Or the Adjuster may not have any close friends, but be so quiet and "good" that no one ever really notices. Either way, the Adjuster tends to avoid close relationships because family experience has shown that close relationships only mean trouble.

If these roles sound like they fit you or someone you know, they may be signalling a problem within the family. The roles are often a way of coping with a problem that otherwise seems out of control. Sometimes people "mix and match," taking on various characteristics from different roles at different times. But underlying the various behaviors are certain feelings that are shared by many people who grew up in homes where there was a problem drinker or drug user.

Effects the Problem Drinker/Drug User Has on You

Al-Anon, an organization for the families, relatives, and friends who feel they have been affected by someone else's drinking, has prepared the following questionnaire to help people identify whether alcoholism (or addiction) affected their childhood or present life.

1. Do you constantly seek approval and affirmation?
2. Do you fail to recognize your accomplishments?

3. Do you fear criticism?
4. Do you overextend yourself?
5. Have you had problems with your own compulsive behavior?
6. Do you have a need for perfection?
7. Are you uneasy when your life is going smoothly, continually anticipating problems?
8. Do you feel more alive in the midst of a crisis?
9. Do you still feel responsible for others, as you did for the problem drinker (or drug user) in your life?
10. Do you care for others easily, yet find it difficult to care for yourself?
11. Do you isolate yourself from other people?
12. Do you respond with anxiety to authority figures and angry people?
13. Do you feel that individuals and society in general are taking advantage of you?
14. Do you have trouble with intimate relationships?
15. Do you confuse pity with love, as you did with the problem drinker?
16. Do you attract and seek people who tend to be compulsive?
17. Do you cling to relationships because you are afraid of being alone?
18. Do you often mistrust your own feelings and the feelings expressed by others?
19. Do you find it difficult to express your emotions?
20. Do you think parental drinking (or drug use) may have affected you?

Members of the family of a problem drinker or drug user tend to want to know where to place the blame. If family members aren't blaming themselves for the addict's problem ("He wouldn't drink if I didn't get him so upset." "She wouldn't take drugs if I had been a better mother."), they are blaming the addict for their problems ("If my mother would just stop drinking, everything would be all right." "I'd do better in school if I didn't have to spend so much time taking care of my druggie brother.").

In fact, families operate as a *system* in which every member's behavior affects every other member's behavior. It is definitely *not* true that the addict is responsible for every bad thing that happens to every member of the family. Nor is it true that any other person but the addict himself or herself is responsible for the excessive drinking or drug taking that may be going on. But it is true that the addict's behavior *affects* every other member of the family, producing the painful and difficult feelings in response. And it is also true that the other members of the family develop patterns of behavior that affect the problem drinker or drug user. This behavior is sometimes spoken of as *enabling*; that is, behavior that *enables* the problem drinker or drug user to continue drinking or taking drugs. Because families of alcoholics or drug users are often drawn into the addict's behavior, family members are sometimes known as "co-alcoholics" or "co-dependents." This means that, without meaning to, they are engaging in behavior that makes it possible for the addict to continue to drink or to take drugs.

For example, let's say that a big family dinner is planned to which relatives are invited. Every member of the family is expected to help clean the house, prepare the dinner, and generally share in the chores associated with the event. Everyone, that is, except the "problem" family member. "Oh, you know how So-and-So is," everyone says. "Can't count on him [her] for anything." This statement may be made in anger, with resignation, or with love, but it always has the same effect: to accept the "problem" behavior of the drinker or drug user, and, by accepting it, to enable it, is to make it possible for the behavior to continue.

Then let's say that the problem drinker or drug user chooses the morning of the family dinner to get seriously drunk or stoned. Everyone springs into action, trying to make sure that the person will be okay by dinner time, so that none of the relatives will know there is a problem. If the parent or child is so drunk or stoned that there is no way the dinner can be held without the problem being noticed, one of the parents calls the relatives to cancel because "someone got sick," or "George was called out of town." Everyone is instructed to say nothing to anyone about what happened, to cover up so that no one knows there is a problem. They may even be asked to pretend to themselves and each other that there is no problem: "Your father is just tired." "Oh, your brother had a bad night last night and he's feeling a little sick today." The problem drinker or drug user is shielded from the consequences of his or her behavior. He or she is allowed to disrupt and control the entire family. Even if family members display angry, punishing behavior toward the "problem" member, still they have agreed with the idea that the member can't help himself/herself. They have agreed that the member is someone who can be expected to constantly disappoint others, to constantly fail or screw up. And they have agreed that, since the member is not able to solve his or her own problems, everyone else must cover up by lying to relatives, taking on extra household chores, and so on.

At the same time that family members are helping the destructive behavior to continue, they may be using that behavior as an excuse for their own problems: "How can I study when my mother is drunk all the time?" "I can't go out on dates because I'm afraid to leave my brother alone in the house." "I can't begin to think about what I'm going to do when I finish school. I know I'll have to stay home to take care of my younger brothers and sisters."

None of this is to say that people with drinking or drug problems are bad people, or that they do not deserve the love of their families. Nor is it to say that you do not have the right to be very, very angry with any family member who is disrupting your life by his or her use of drugs or alcohol. The point is not to blame anyone, but for you to figure out what kind of behavior you *can* control—your own—and what kind of behavior you *can't* control—that of the drinker or drug user.

Coping with a Family Member's Drug or Alcohol Dependency

What are some of the ways that you can cope with the drug or alcohol dependency of another member of the family? The first step is to separate your behavior from theirs. Accept that you can't get the other person to stop drinking, and that you are not responsible for his or her decision to continue drinking (or using drugs).

Of course, this is easier said than done. After all, you have had years of practice wishing and hoping that you could do something to make things "all right." Accepting that you *cannot* make things all right for someone you love is one of the hardest things you'll ever have to do in life. It may take you a while to believe that even though you cannot make things all right for the drinker or drug user, you can make things all right for you. If you can put the energy you've been using to cover up the other person's behavior, to pretend that nothing is wrong or to be angry, into figuring out how to get the help *you* need and how to make things better for *you*, you'll be on your way. Even if this sounds hard, at least try out this new way of thinking. Practice stopping yourself whenever you think "If only he/she would stop . . ." or "I can't do _____ because of so-and-so." Turn those thoughts toward solving a problem: "Where can I find the help that I need to get what I want? If I can't turn to my parents, whom can I turn to?"

The next step is to recognize that the alcoholic or drug user has two main weapons against everyone in the family. The first is the power to make everyone angry. The second is the power to make everybody anxious. Because other family members do love the alcoholic/drug user, they are concerned and anxious about him or her; because the alcoholic/drug user is engaged in destructive behavior, he or she can make everyone angry. However, if you allow your addicted family member to succeed, to make you angry or to make you anxious, the addict can use your anger to justify his or her own feelings of self-hatred. "See, even my own son/daughter/brother/sister thinks I'm a jerk, and I probably am. Everybody hates me. I'd better have another drink/another hit to take my mind off of it." Likewise, the addict can use your anxiety to prove to him- or herself that failure is inevitable. If, for example, worried family members cover a bad check written by someone with a drug or drinking problem because they are worried about the addict and don't want him or her to go to jail, they have not really solved the problem. They have only proven to the addict that he or she needn't solve problems or face the consequences of irresponsible actions. The addict realizes that other family members will "help" him or her by dealing with the bad consequences of the addiction themselves. Neither getting angry nor getting anxious is helpful to the family member with a drinking or drug problem.

Again, it may be difficult giving up your anger and your anxiety. You have probably spent years worrying about this family member and how his or her behavior will affect you. You have probably been angry for years at the way this person is disrupting your life. You have a right to both of these feelings. Each is understandable. However, if you give in to them, you won't really be changing anything for yourself. Hard as it may sound, in order to change your own situation, *you* will have to change the way *you* respond to the person who is drinking or taking drugs.

What is helpful—both to the family member concerned and to you—is to try and remain *detached*. Detachment means that you don't participate in another's addiction. You take yourself out of the way when behavior that you don't like is being displayed, but you don't evaluate or judge the other person. You find ways not to suffer because of the actions of the addicted person, not to allow yourself to be used or abused by someone else, not to do for others what they should do for themselves, not to cover up for another person's mistakes or misdeeds, not to create a crisis, and not to prevent a crisis if it occurs.

The way to arrive at detachment is to begin with yourself. Instead of wishing that the family member would get help with his or her problem, *you* get help with your problem. Find a support group, a therapist, one of the anonymous groups, or some other form of support outside your family. (See appendix, page 85.) Figure out ways that you can pursue your goals in school or in other activities that don't depend on the disruptive family member. Look for friendships that are *not* based on lying or covering up for someone, that encourage you to be honest about your feelings, including your feelings about your family. Ask a counselor, a librarian, an anonymous group, or someone listed under Mental Health Services in the *Yellow Pages* for books or pamphlets to read about alcohol or drugs so you can understand some other ways to think about the behavior of the drinker or drug-taker in your family.

Do these suggestions make you angry or extremely nervous? Are you thinking, "I *can't* go on with my life, because So-and-So has spoiled it!" or "Oh, fine, I'll make all these efforts to fix things, but I bet So-and-So will find a way to ruin it, so what's the use?" Or perhaps you're thinking, "I can't tell anyone about my feelings about my father/mother/brother/sister—we don't talk about our family's problems in public," or "If I went to a counselor, then everyone would know my dad had a problem and I couldn't do that to him."

If you find that any talk about what you can do with your own life upsets you, that's not surprising. You've had years of practice, years of being told that you *can't* do anything until this other person lets you, years of being told that it's your job to make everything all right. But if you are old enough to read this page and think about what you read, you are old enough to think about trying to get help for yourself. It may not be fair that you should have to work so hard, it may be frightening or upsetting, but it *is* a choice that you have. Your other choice is to hope that some other person changes—and that's something you have no control over.

If you learn all you can about alcoholism and drug addiction, and about ways that you can change your own behavior to make *yourself* happy, you may have a better chance of helping the alcoholic or drug user in your family. More importantly, even if that family member never changes, you will have gone ahead and made the choices that *you* wanted for your own life. You will have escaped the control of the addict over your life by accepting responsibility for your own actions and refusing responsibility for the actions of another.

The following suggestions are adapted from Al-Anon's guide to family members of alcoholics, but they are also useful for members of families with other addiction problems.

1. Learn all the facts about how alcoholism/addiction affects people and their families and put them to work in your own life. Don't start trying to help the alcoholic—start trying to help yourself.
2. Attend the meetings of some support group, such as Alateen or Narateen (for the teen members of families of narcotics users). If possible, go to a mental health clinic, or to a competent counselor who understands the problems of families with addicts.
3. Remember that you are emotionally involved with the addict in your family. Changing your own attitude toward the person, and your own approach to the problem can be helpful both to you and to the other person.
4. Encourage all the beneficial activities of the alcoholic or drug user, such as his or her participation in A.A., therapy, or some other support group. Cooperate in these activities.
5. Learn that love cannot exist without justice, so that you don't have to confuse loving someone with accepting his or her abuse. If someone abuses you, you don't have to accept it, no matter how much you love the person.
6. Don't lecture, blame, argue, or threaten the addict in your family. Don't lose your temper. Don't cover up the consequences of drinking or drug use. You may feel better for a while, but the situation will be worse.
7. Don't let your anxiety make you do for the family member what he or she should do for him/herself.
8. Don't let the alcoholic or drug user take advantage of you;

that's just a way of helping him or her avoid responsibility.

9. Don't put off facing the reality that alcoholism and drug addiction are illnesses that only get worse with time. You have a right to be happy in your life. Find the help that you need so that you can get on with your own life, whatever your family member does.

Sometimes when family members follow these suggestions, the alcoholic or drug-dependent family member is helped to give up his or her addiction. Sometimes not. Whatever the other person does, however, you can move forward in your own life by making the choices that are right for you.

More information about Alateen, Narateen, and other support groups is available in the appendix. If you are the relative or friend of someone with a drug or drinking problem, you should strongly consider joining one of these groups. It is very difficult to make changes by yourself. Everyone needs the support of others who share the same problems and who know what you are going through. These groups are confidential, and usually don't even use last names so that the identity of parents or relatives is also protected.

Some Final Thoughts

If there's one message you should take away from this book, it's that there is always something you can do to make your life better, that you *can* make good choices that will work for you. Ultimately, you are the one who will choose what your relationship to drugs and alcohol will be.

Of course, this doesn't mean that you can choose to drink heavily and never feel hungover, or that you can choose to do crack regularly and never become addicted. The reason for going into the facts about drugs and alcohol in so much detail is to make clear that your choices will have consequences. Understanding the consequences is part of making good choices.

You should also be aware that many others are in situations like yours—whatever your situation is. The statistics in this book should make it clear that there are many people who do not drink or take drugs, and there are also many who do. There are millions of people who don't have a problem with drinking or drugs, either because they stay away from alcohol and chemicals or because they deal with those substances in such a way as not to lose control over their behavior. There are also millions of people who do have a problem with drinking or drugs, people who take one drink and can't stop, or who consistently use drugs to avoid facing problems when they would be happier just solving the problem, people whose use of liquor or drugs leads them to lose control over their lives.

Knowing that you are not alone should make it easier to make your own choices, to stick to them if they work and change them if they don't work. Knowing that you are not alone should also make it easier to get help, if you need it.

The stories of those who have gone to drug treatment centers or through the anonymous programs show that recovery from an addiction is not easy—but it can be done. Recovery is not easy, because it involves facing things that you have been trying to cover up for a long time. Often people drink or take drugs because they are trying to escape from feelings that are painful, frightening, or unpleasant. They may have difficulties that they believe they cannot cope with. There may be painful things in their families that are difficult to deal with. When you begin to look at something you have avoided facing for a long time, it's easy to feel frightened, helpless, or discouraged.

Many treatment centers or other programs seem difficult to get involved with because they demand that the drinker or drug user take responsibility for his or her life. Since these people often drink or take drugs because they feel out of control, it can be tough for them to take back responsibility for their lives by not drinking/using drugs.

In addition, treatment centers, anonymous programs, and other forms of therapy may shake up established life patterns. You may find that while you were drinking or taking drugs, you chose friends who would support that behavior. If you want to change your behavior, you may run into resistance from your friends. They will either have to change with you or accept the way you were before your addiction.

Likewise, your family may be used to your drinking or drug taking. Even though they may have been giving you a lot of grief for your "bad" behavior, they were used to it. When you begin to change, they must begin to change. No longer can they blame everything on *your* problem, feel superior to you, or enjoy helping you out of a bad time. You won't be having the same kind of difficulties—so they may not know what to expect or how to behave. Some people even feel that their families wish they would start drinking or doing drugs again because that is more familiar, even if it is not pleasant, and everyone already knows what to expect!

These are the difficulties that you will face if you have a problem with liquor or drugs and decide to do something about it. But the rewards are definitely far, far greater than the difficulties. People who have stopped drinking or taking drugs talk about being able to live again, whereas before they felt numb or dead. Recovered addicts or drinkers begin to see how much energy they spent trying *not* to have bad feelings—but that didn't mean they succeeded.

People who are recovering from an addiction also talk about the wonderful freedom from fear and anxiety. For the first time in years, they are facing their problems, rather than running away from them. There is a huge relief in finally looking your problems in the eye, instead of fearing them so much you constantly look for a way out. This is not to say that once you stop drinking or taking drugs in an out-of-control way you will never be frightened again. It is to say that a lot of things that used to frighten you will stop seeming dangerous or even very important.

That's because you'll have a much more realistic sense of your own power and your own worth. People who drink or take drugs often feel helpless and worthless; they drink or take drugs to make those feelings go away. Since those good feelings last only as long as the high—and sometimes not even that long—the bad feelings seem even stronger when they return. If you have had a problem with drinking or drugs, you may have experienced mood swings such as feeling like you can do anything to feeling like you can't do anything. (Unfortunately, these mood swings are also a normal part of life—especially teenage life! But they are more extreme and more unrealistic for drinkers and drug users who are using chemicals to escape.)

If this has been your pattern, you have not realized how powerful you really are, or how to measure your own worth. You may feel that if you aren't perfect, you aren't worth anything, or that one mistake confirms your suspicions that you really are no good. Part of recovering from an addiction will be learning that you can be powerful *and* make mistakes, be worthy *and* do an occasional bad thing. You will be able to enjoy your feelings of power and worthiness, rather than seeing them destroyed each time you make a mistake or have a setback.

Perhaps the best part of your recovery will be the sense of all the new possibilities that open up to you. If you are letting your life be ruled by drugs or alcohol, you aren't even able to look at all the possibilities for your life. If you accept responsibility for your own life, you begin to see all sorts of things that you can do that you never thought about doing. You suddenly have the energy to go after the things you want, instead of simply running away from the things that feel too hard to handle.

Remember that there is help out there if you need it, and that if you keep working at it, you can make the changes you want. And what you learn about yourself as you make your choices about drugs and alcohol will stand you in good stead for the rest of your life.

Appendix
Where to Find Help

If you think you or one of your friends or a family member has a problem with drugs or alcohol, you can find help by contacting one of the following organizations or agencies listed here. They are divided into four sections:

I Drug and Alcohol Facilities. (Pages 86-133.) These are programs specifically designed for teenagers who may need help on an in-patient or out-patient basis. They are listed geographically.

II Alcoholics Annonymous Intergroups. (Pages 134-137.) These are listings of main offices of Alcoholics Anonymous in your state. They will be able to supply you with a list of places or people you can contact to get help through local A.A. meetings. They are listed geographically.

III Al-Anon or Alateen. (Page 137.) Al-Anon is an organization to help anyone whose life has been deeply affected by close association with an alcoholic. Alateen is a division of Al-Anon; its goal is identical, and it is only for teenagers.
Al-Anon or Alateen
World Service Office
P.O. Box 862
Midtown Station
New York, New York 10018-0862

IV State Authorities. (Pages 137-139.) These are listings of state offices that are involved in referring people to agencies, organizations, hospitals, or programs that deal with alcohol or drug abuse.

I   Drug and Alcohol Facilities

ALABAMA

Addictive Disease Program
Elmore County Hospital
1201 Company Street
Wetumpka, AL 36092
(205) 567-4311, Ext. 330
Epsie Hagan

Brookwood/Parkside Lodge
   Birmingham
P.O. Box 128
Warrior, AL 35180
(205) 647-1945
Morris Hamilton

Brookwood/Parkside Lodge Mobile
P.O. Box 850759
Malaga Station
Mobile, AL 36691-1174
(203) 633-0906
Jerry Crowder

CareUnit Hospital Program
Lloyd Noland Hospital
701 Ridgeway Road
Fairfield, AL 35064
(205) 783-5156

Charter Pines Recovery Center
251 Cox Street
Mobile, Al 36604
(205) 432-8811
Wayne Fields
Charter Counseling
Outpt. (205) 432-8811

Charter Woods Hospital
700 Cottonwood Road
Dothan, AL 36301
(205) 793-6660
Jack Boswell

Grays Landing Substance Abuse
   Treatment Center
Rt. 1, Box 33F
Sheffield, AL 35660
(205) 383-1092
Tommy Pirkle

ALASKA

Charter North Hospital
2530 DeBarr Road
P.O. Box 143929
Anchorage, AK 99514
(907) 258-7575
John Sankey

Milam Recovery Centers of Alaska
4426 Wright Street
Anchorage, AK 99507
(907) 562-6687
Andrew J. Brennan

Phillip Alcoholism
Treatment Center
P.O. Box 388
Bethel, AK 99559
(907) 543-2129
George Ives

Seward Life Action Council
Alcohol, Mental Health & Human
  Services
502 Adams Street
P.O. Box 5257
Seward, AK 99964
(907) 224-5257
Dennis M. Scholl, Ph.D.,
Program Director

ARIZONA

Alcoholism Council of Tucson
2222 N. Craycroft, Ste. E
Tucson, AZ 85712
(602) 795-8983
Don Jogensen

Camelback Hospitals
Crises & Information Service
7575 E. Earll Drive
Scottsdale, AZ 85251
(602) 253-1334
(800) 253-1334
Jim Hight, MC, NCC, Dir.
Referral Service

Camelback Hospital
Phoenix
5055 N. 34th Street
Phoenix, AZ 85018
(602) 955-6200
Ron Null, MSW, Dir.

Camelback Hospital
Sedona Villa
P.O. Box 4245
West Sedona, AZ 86340
(800) 548-3008
(800) 874-9070 (AZ)
James Deem, MBA

Camelback Hospital
Scottsdale
7575 E. Earll Drive
Scottsdale, AZ 85251
(602) 941-7500
Kit Wilson, MSW

Camelback Hospital
Wendy Treatment Center
1300 N. 77th Street
Scottsdale, AZ 85257
(602) 945-7999
Mike Todd

Camelback Hospital
West Valley
5625 W. Thunderbird Road
Glendale, AZ 85306
(602) 588-4700
Gerald Mayer, Ph.D.

CIGNA Healthplan
Alcohol/Drug Dependency Program
755 E. McDowell Road
Phoenix, AZ 85006
(602) 271-5239
Dr. Kevin Wandler
Medical Director

HCA Sonora Desert Hospital
Alcohol & Drug Treatment Program
1920 W. Rudasill
Tucson, AZ 85741
(602) 297-5500
Adult Program Director

O'Reilly Care Center at Green Valley
75 W. Calle de las Tiendas
#103B
Green Valley, AZ 85614
(602) 625-2944
Paul Hilton

Sierra Tucson
P.O. Box 8307
Tucson, AZ 85738
(602) 624-4000
(800) 624-9001
Judy Schelb

St. Luke's Behavioral Health Center
  Chemical Dependency Services
1800 E. Van Buren
Phoenix AZ 85006
(602) 251-8535
Dennis A. Armstrong

Terros, Inc. Chemical Dependency
   Programs
4545 N. 27th Avenue
Phoenix, AZ 85017
(602) 249-1749 (24-Hrs.)
Ilene Dode

Westcenter Institute
3838 N. Campbell Avenue
Tucson, AZ 85719
(602) 327-5431
Jacquelyn St. Germaine

ARKANSAS

CareUnit Hospital Program
Arkansas Rehabilitation Institute
9601 Interstate 630, Exit 7
Little Rock, AR 72205-7249
(501) 223-7507

CareUnit Hospital Program
Sparks Regional Medical Center
4th Floor West
1311 South I Street
Fort Smith, AR 72901
(501) 441-5500

Charter Vista Hospital
4253 Crossover Road
Fayetteville, AR 72701
(501) 521-5731
Tim Herr

Crowley Ridge Development Council
   Inc. Alcohol & Drug Programs
249 S. Main Street
Jonesboro, AR 72401
(501) 935-8610
Bob Yopp, Director

Decision Point Substance Abuse
   Programs
215 Club Inc.
P.O. Box 1174
Springdale, AR 72765-1174
(501) 756-1060
Steve Sargent

Newton House
301 Walter Street
Hot Springs, AR 71901
(501) 321-9079
Gary Hardin

Quapaw House, Inc.
400 Quapaw Street
Hot Springs, AR 71901
(501) 624-1360
Gary Hardin

CALIFORNIA

Alta Vista Hospital
301 E. Roberts Lane
Bakersfield, CA 93308
(805) 393-3000
Fenton Karnes
Program Director

Avanti Non-Residential Treatment
   Services
1551 E. Shaw, Suite 103
Fresno, CA 93710
(209) 442-3900
Denny Kimalehto

CareUnit Hospital of Los Angeles
5035 Coliseum Street
Los Angeles, CA 90016
(213) 295-6441

CareUnit Hospital Program
Community Hospital of Sacramento
2251 Hawthorne Street
Sacramento, CA 95815
(916) 920-1507

CareUnit Hospital Program
Crossroads Hospital
6323 Woodman Avenue
Van Nuys, CA 91401
(818) 782-2470

CareUnit Hospital Program
Glendale Adventist Medical Center
Chevy Chase
801 W. Chevy Chase Drive
Glendale, CA 91205
(818) 247-9303

CareUnit Hospital Program
Goleta Valley Community Hospital
351 S. Patterson
Santa Barbara, CA 93160-6306
(805) 683-5747

CareUnit Hospital Program
Marshal Hale Memorial Hospital
3773 Sacramento Street
San Francisco, CA 94188
(415) 666-7867

CareUnit Hospital Program
Palmdale Hospital Medical Center
1212 E. Avenue 'S'
Palmdale, CA 93550
(805) 265-6410

CareUnit Hospital Program
San Bernardino Community Hospital
1500 W. 17th Street
San Bernardino, CA 92411
(714) 887-8111

CareUnit Hospital Program
San Jose Hospital
675 E. Santa Clara Street
San Jose, CA 95112
(408) 279-CARE

Centinela Hospital
Medical Center Lifestarts
555 E. Hardy Street
Inglewood, CA 90301
(213) 677-4357
Jackie Mills

Charter Pacific Hospital
4025 W. 226th Street
Torrance, CA 90505
(213) 373-7733
Ken Guy

CIGNA Healthplan of Calif.
Department of Chemical
    Dependency
1711 W. Temple Street
Los Angeles, CA 90026
(213) 484-3015
Sanford M. Reder, M.D.

Clovis Community Hospital/ARC
88 North Dewitt
Clovis, CA 93612
(209) 442-3940
Bud Taylor

Coldwater Canyon Hospital
A Life Plus Facility
6421 Coldwater Canyon Avenue
North Hollywood, CA 91606
(818) 769-1000
Ruth Sherwood

College Hospital
10802 College Place
Cerritos, CA 90701
(213) 924-9581
Barry Weiss

College Hospital Amethyst
(Women's) & Men's Program
10802 College Place
Cerritos, CA 90701
(213) 924-9581
Janet Cullen

Community Behavioral Health Group,
    Inc.
6580 Brockton Avenue
Suite 103
Riverside, CA 92506
(714) 784-3050
Mark Thuve

Desert Alcoholism Coalition/The
    Hayman Center
Palm Springs, CA 92262
(619) 323-1721
Beverly Midgley

Forest Farm Chemical Dependency
  Recovery Program
P.O. Box 279
Forest Knolls, CA 94933
(415) 488-9287
Barbara George

Gladman Memorial Hospital Alcohol/
  Drug Treatment
2633 E. 27th Street
Oakland, CA 94601
(415) 536-8111
Maurice Kamens, Dir.

HCA Woodview-Calabasas Hospital
  Substance Abuse Treatment Services
25100 Calabasas Road
Calabasas, CA 91302
(818) 888-7500
Substance Abuse Coordinator

Health Care Medical Center of Tustin
14662 Newport Avenue
Tustin, CA 92681
(714) 838-9600, Ext. 4000
Ella May Green

Manor West Hospital Alcohol/Drug
  Abuse Program
1231 South Alvarado Street
Los Angeles, CA 90006
(213) 387-3143
(818) 981-3198
Ronnie Brown/Ledi Moret

Memorial Coastview
Memorial Medical Center
2801 Atlantic Avenue
P.O. Box 1428
Long Beach, CA 90801
(213) 426-6619
Steve Brodie

Monte Villa Hospital
Alcohol & Drug Treatment Program
17925 Halle Avenue
P.O. Box 947
Morgan Hill, CA 95027
(408) 226-3020
William P. Macaskille
Dir., Program Development

New Beginnings at Community
  Hospital at Los Gatos
815 Pollard Road
Los Gatos, CA 95030
(408) 378-6141
Lani Clark

New Beginnings at Doctors Hospital of
  Lakewood
5300 N. Clark Avenue
Lakewood, CA 90712
(213) 866-9711
Barbara Elvgren/Cheryl Kosiba

New Beginnings at Modesto City
  Hospital
730 17th Street
Modesto, CA 95354
(209) 577-1000
Debbi Bailey

New Beginnings at Placentia Linda
  Community Hospital
1301 Rose Drive
Placentia, CA 92670
(714) 524-4894
JoAnn Hahn

Pasadena Community Hospital
1845 N. Fair Oaks Avenue
Pasadena, CA 91103
(818) 798-7811
Joanne Trejo

Phoenix Program
Redlands Community Hospital
350 Terracina Boulevard
Redlands, CA 92373
(714) 793-3101
Michael VanNess, Director

Phoenix Program
Sonoma Valley Hospital
347 Andrieux Street
Sonoma, CA 95476
(707) 996-6500
Terry Rooney, Director

Recovery Alliance at San Pedro
  Peninsula Hospital
1300 W. Seventh Street
San Pedro, CA 90732
(213) 832-3111
Michael Lucid

Riverside Co. Dept. of Mental Health
  Desert Drug Program
134 E. Hobson Way, Ste. 5
Blythe, CA 92225
(619) 922-9111
Receptionist

Robert F. Kennedy Medical Chemical
  Dependency Program
4500 W. 116th Street
Hawthorne, CA 90250
(213) 970-0630
Larry Jacobson, Adm. Dir.

Scripps Memorial Hospital
McDonald Center
9904 Genessee Avenue
La Jolla, CA 92037
(800) 382-HELP
(619) 458-4300
Jacque Spratling

Sobriety Brings A Change Substance
  Abuse Program
2214 21st Street
Sacramento, CA 95818
(916) 454-4242
Joe Ganaway, Executive Director

St. Joseph Medical Center Alcohol &
  Chemical Dependency Service
Buena Vista & Alameda Streets
Burbank, CA 91505
(818) 843-5111, Ext. 7688
James Conway, Director

Starting Point
Vesper Hospital
22455 Maple Court
Hayward, CA 94541
(415) 537-7714

Steps, Inc.
3533 Mount Vernon Avenue
Bakersfield, CA 93306
(805) 871-3353
Vincent S. Raj

United Health Plan/Enrolle Employee
  Assistance Program
3405 W. Imperial Highway
Inglewood, CA 90303
(213) 671-3465
Leonard Westmorland

COLORADO

AMI-St. Luke's Addictions Recovery
  Unit
601 E. 19th Avenue
Denver, CO 80203
(303) 869-2280
Phil Waggoner

The Ark/The Alcohol Recovery Center
P.O. Box 626
Green Mountain Falls, CO 80819
(303) 684-9483
J. Michael Pattison

Aurora Center for Treatment
Alcoholism Drug Programs
Outpatient
15400 E. 14th Place
Suite 433
Aurora, CO 80011
(303) 344-9750 or
Denver (303) 329-0621
Bobbi Thompson, Director
CANX

CareUnit Hospital Program
Mercy Medical Center
1650 Filmore Street
Denver, CO 80206
(303) 393-3500

Cedar Springs Hospital
2135 Southgate Road
Colorado Springs, CO 80906
(303) 633-4114
Kathy Cox

The Centre at Porter Hospital
2525 S. Downing Street
Denver, CO 80210
(303) 778-5774
Larry Gibson, M.D., Medical Director

Durango Aru
3801 N. Main Avenue
Durango, CO 81301
(303) 259-6151
Scott Wallace/Bill Ball

Gateway Treatment Center
   Alcoholism/Drug Treatment
1191 S. Parker Road
Suite 100
Denver, CO 80231
(303) 696-8407 (24 Hrs.)
Paul Staley

Midwestern Colorado Mental Health
   Center
447 N. 3rd Street
Montrose, CO 81402
(303) 249-6058
Dr. Joseph Price

New Beginnings at Denver
1325 Everett Court
Lakewood, CO 80215
(303) 231-9090
William McCabe

New Beginnings at Fort Collins
1225 Redwood Street
Fort Collins, CO 80524
(303) 493-3389
Cam Pratt

Parkside Lodge of Colorado, Inc.
8801 Lipan Street
Thornton, CO 80221
(303) 320-0800
Ron Drier

Parkview Chemical Dependency
   Program
56 Club Manor
Pueblo, CO 81008
(303) 584-4343
Dr. Wallce E. Smith, Ph.D.

Whole Person Health Center
999 Alpine Avenue
Boulder, CO 80302
(303) 449-4121
Darvin W. Smith

CONNECTICUT

Farrell Treatment Center
586 Main Street
New Britain, CT 06051
(203) 225-4641
Richard Ranaudo, Dir.

Hall-Brooke Hospital
Division of Hall-Brooke Foundation
47 Long Lots Road
Westport, CT 06881
(203) 227-1251, Ext. 222
Adminis. Officer

Natchaug Hospital
189 Storrs Road
Mansfield Center, CT 06250
(203) 423-1673
Substance Abuse Services Director

Parkside Lodge of Connecticut, Inc.
Rt. 7, Box 668
Canaan, CT 06018
(203) 824-5426
John Reese

Rockville General Hospital Human
   Services & Alcohol Treatment
31 Union Street
Rockville, CT 06066
(203) 872-0501, Ext. 297
G. (Smokey) Orcutt

Silver Hill Foundation
P.O. Box 1117
New Canaan, CT 06840
(203) 966-3561
Carlotta Schuster, M.D.

St. Mary's Hospital
Joseph Center
56 Franklin Street
Waterbury, CT 06702
(203) 574-6083
Samuel R. Segal, M.A., C.A.C.

Vitam Center, Inc.
P.O. Box 730
Norwalk, CT 06852
(203) 846-2091
Dr. Leonard Kenewitz

Wakeman Hall at the Children's Center
Adolescent & Alcoholism & Drug
   Treatment Center
1400 Whitney Avenue
Hamden, CT 06517
(203) 248-2116
Peter B. Rockholz, MSSW, Director

The Wheeler Clinic, Inc.
Specializing Drug/Alcohol Treatment
91 Northwest Drive
Plainville, CT 06062
(203) 747-6801
Joseph Puzzo, Dir.

DELAWARE

Brandywine Counseling & Diagnostic
   Center
305 W. 12th Street
Wilmington, DE 19801
(302) 656-2348
David Skinner, Executive Director

Delaware Alcohol & Drug Treatment
   Center
Individual & Family
1606 W. 16th Street
Wilmington, DE 19806
(302) 656-4044
Dr. Frank M. Matthews, Executive
   Director

Greenwood 28-Day Treatment with
   Detox
1000 Old Lancaster Pike
Hockessen, DE 19707
(302) 239-3410
Richard P. Sanger

HCA Greenwood
1000 Old Lancaster Pike
Hockessen, DE 19707
(302) 239-3410
Program Director

FLORIDA

Addictions & Family Health
4300 S.W. 13th Street
Gainesville, FL 32608
(904) 374-5690
Ronnie Wright

Adolescent Addiction Treatment
  Program
1861 N.W. South River Drive
Miami, FL 33125
(305) 642-3555
Robert Gray

Anon Anew at Boca Raton
2600 N.W. Fifth Avenue
Boca Raton, FL 33431
(305) 368-6222
Dan Sullivan

Apalachee Community Mental Health
  Services, Inc.
625 E. Tennessee
P.O. Box 1782
Tallahassee, FL 32302
(904) 487-2930
Paul Cromwell

Bayshore on the Gulf
1346 Bayshore Boulevard
Dunedin, FL 33528
(813) 733-0421

The Beachcomber Family Center
4493 N. Ocean Boulevard
Delray Beach, FL 33444
(305) 734-1818
James A. Bryan

Bowling Green Inn
US 17 N.P.O. Box 337
Bowling Green, FL 33834
(813) 375-2218
Linda Todd, Exec. Dir./Charles Adams

CareUnit of Coral Springs
3275 N.W. 99th Way
Coral Springs, FL 33065
(305) 753-5200

CareUnit of Jacksonville Beach
1320 Roberts Drive
Jacksonville Beach, FL 33250
(904) 241-5133

Charter Glade Hospital
6900 Colonial Blvd., S.E.
Ft. Myers, FL 33912
(813) 939-0403
Admitting Office

The Cloisters at Pine Island
Waterfront Drive
P.O. Box 1616
Pineland, FL 33945-1616
(813) 283-1019
Michel F. Doherty, M.H.S., C.A.C.

Community Out-Reach Services, Inc.
442 E. New York Avenue
Box 597
Deland, FL 32721
(904) 736-0420
Steve Segner

Cornerstone Institute, Inc.
Outpatient Treatment
624 Maitland Avenue
Altamonte Springs, FL 32701
(305) 830-8808
Stefan Johannsson

Disc Village Treatment Center
P.O. Box 568
Woodville, FL 32362
(904) 421-4115
Kerry White

Fair Oaks Hospital at Boca Delray
5440 Linton Blvd.
Delray Beach, FL 33445-651
(305) 495-3737
Karin Hilton

Gateway Community Services
Gateway Plaza
1833 Blvd., Suite 507
Jacksonville, FL 32206
(904) 356-0000

Glenbeigh of Tampa
3102 138th Avenue E.
(813) 971-5000
Robert Denson

The Grove Counseling Center
580 Old Sanford
Oviedo Road
Winter Springs, FL 32708
(305) 327-1765
Larry Visser

HCA West Lake Hospital
Alcohol/Drug Abuse Program
589 W. Sanlando Springs Dr.
Longwood, FL 32750
(305) 834-0900
Program Coordinator

Heritage-Jensen Beach
2065 N.E. Indian River Dr.
Jensen Beach, FL 33457
(305) 334-5566
David Durick, Exec. Dir.

Heritage-Sebastian Human Hospital
Sebastian
P.O. Box 957
Sebastian, FL 32958
(305) 589-0308
Nollie Robinson, Program
Director of the Chemical
Dependency Unit

Human Hospital
Daytona Beach Help Unit
400 N. Clyde Morris Blvd.
Daytona Beach, FL 32020
(904) 252-4357
Toni Barrett

Humana Hospital
S. Brow. Chemical Dependency Center
5100 W. Hallandale Beach Blvd.
Hollywood, FL 33023
(305) 966-8100
Ron West

Intervention Associates of Sarasota
2975 Bee Ridge Road
Suite D
Sarasota, FL 33579
(813) 923-2326
Robert Stenza

Koala Center
Highway 476 W.
P.O. Box 250
Bushnesll, FL 33513
(904) 793-6000
Susan A. Yates,
Executive Director

Koala Outreach
University Professional Center
3500 E. Fletcher Avenue
Suite 531
Tampa, FL 33612
(813) 972-4423
Valerie Feingold

Lake Hospital STAR Program
1710 4th Avenue North
Lake Worth, FL 33460
(305) 588-7341

Medfield Center Alcohol/Drug
   Treatment Center
12891 Seminole Boulevard
Largo, FL 33544
(813) 581-8757
Hanzel Pereira, M.A., C.R.C.

Miami Mental Health Center
Substance Abuse Unit
2141 W. 1st Street
Miami, FL 33135
(305) 643-1660
Silvia Quintana

Palmview Hospital
2510 N. Florida Avenue
Lakeland, FL 33805
(813) 682-6105
(800) 282-3480
Steve Pasky

Pinellas Comprehensive Alcohol
   Services, Inc. (PCAS)
6150 150th Avenue North
Clearwater, FL 33520
(813) 530-1417
Cesar M. Perez, M.S.W., Executive
   Director

Recovery Alternatives, Inc.
660 Shoreview Avenue
Winter Park, FL 32789
(305) 644-4033
Scott Gandert

The Starting Place—Comp. Mental
   Health Services
Adolescent Substance Abuse
2057 Coolidge Street
Hollywood, FL 33020
(305) 925-2225
Sheldon Shaffer, Program Director

Storefront Centers, Inc.
1670 Main Street
Sarasota, FL 33577
(813) 953-3595
James Sleepen

Sun Coast Hospital
2025 Indian Rock Road
Largo, FL 34294-202
(813) 585-9986
Kathy Molinaro

GEORGIA

The Bradley Center, Inc.
2000 Sixteenth Avenue
Columbus, GA 31993
(404) 324-4882
Robin Terry, RN

Brawner Psychiatric Institute
   Recovery Center
3180 Atlanta Street, S.E.
Smyrna, GA 30080
(404) 436-0081
Claudette Dunkin

Charter Brook Hospital for Adolescent
   Chemical Dependency Treatment
3913 N. Peachtree Road
Atlanta, GA 30341
(404) 457-8315
Assessment Center

Charter by the Sea Hospital
2927 Demere Road
St. Simons Island, GA 31522
(912) 638-1999
Jane Walker, R.N.

Charter Lake Hospital
3500 Riverside Drive
Macon, GA 31210
(912) 474-6200
Al Stines

Cobb-Douglas Mental Health Center
6133 Love Street
Austell, GA 30001
(404) 941-2416
David Smith

Coliseum Psychiatric Hospital
Addictions Recovery Unit
340 Hospital Drive
Macon, GA 31208
(912) 741-1355
Philip R. Wetherington, Director

Greenleaf Center, Inc.
Substance Abuse Program
500 Greenleaf Circle
Ft. Oglethorpe, GA 30742
(404) 861-4357
(800) 982-9922
John Tallman

Greenleaf Center, Inc.
Substance Abuse Program
2209 Pineview Drive
Valdosta, GA 31602
(912) 247-4357
(800) 247-2747
Diana Dunten

HCA Coliseum Psychiatric Hospital
  Addiction Recovery Program
340 Hospital Drive
Macon, GA 31208
(912) 741-1355
Program Director

Koala Center of Jefferson Hospital
1067 Peachtree Street
Louisville, GA 30434
(912) 625-7949
Roger Gardner

Metro Atlanta Recovery Residences,
  Inc.
P.O. Box 85
Clarkson, GA 30021
(404) 872-4913
Donnie D. Brown

Ridgeview Institute
3995 S. Cobb Drive
Smyrna, GA 30080
(404) 434-4567
Kay Whaley

Turning Point
P.O. Box 1177
Moutrie, GA 31768
(912) 985-4815
(800) 342-1075 (GA)
Gary Bulkin
Transportation Available
(800) 847-5822

Willingway Hospital
311 Jones Mill Road
Statesboro, GA 30458
(912) 764-6236
Toll Free (800) 235-0790
In GA (800) 242-4040
Al J. Mooney, III, M.D.

Woodridge Hospital
The Center for Addictive Diseases
P.O. Box 1764, Germany Rd.
Clayton, GA 30525
(404) 782-3100
Lou Kuntz

HAWAII

Alcoholic Rehabilitation Services of
  Hawaii-Hina
Mauka Program
P.O. Box G
Kaneohe, HI 96744
(808) 235-4531
John Eichnor

Castle Alcoholism & Addictions
  Program
640 Ulukahiki
Kailua, HI 96734
(808) 263-4429
Tina Dameron

Kahi Mohala Hospital
91-2301 Fort Weaver Road
Ewa Beach, HI 96706
(808) 671-8511
(800) 531-5145
Karen Cornell

IDAHO

Alcoholism Treatment Unit
State Hospital North
P.O. Box 672
Orofino, ID 83544
(208) 476-4513
Program Director

Walker Act Center
1120 Montana
Gooding, ID 83330-054
(208) 934-8461

ILLINOIS

Addiction Recovery of Chicago
1776 Moon Lake Boulevard
Hoffman Estates, IL 60194
(800) 423-9814
In IL (800) 942-0541
Mike Breen

Alcoholism Drug Abuse Treatment
   Center
St. Mary's Hospital
1800 E. Lakeshore Drive
Decatur, IL 62521
(217) 429-2963
Janet A. Harper, Director

Alexian Brothers Medical Center
Alcoholism Treatment Center
800 W. Biesterfield
Elk Grove Village, IL 60007
(312) 981-3524
Barry Komie

Belleville Mental Health Center
Al-Lirt Alcohol Out-Patient Program
200 N. Illinois
Belleville, IL 62220
(618) 235-8100
John Henry, Ph.D.

BroMann HealthCare's Chemical
   Dependence Unit
Brokaw Hospital
Normal, IL 61761
(309) 454-1400, Ext. 434
Gerald Rehagen

CareUnit Hospital Program
Glenbrook Hospital
2100 Pfingsten Road
Glenview, IL 60025
(312) 729-5020

CareUnit Hospital Program
St. Elizabeth Hospital
1431 N. Claremont Avenue
Chicago, IL 60622
(312) 278-5015

CareUnit Hospital Program
St. Joseph Hospital
915 E. Fifth Street
Alton, IL 62002
(618) 463-5655

CareUnit Hospital Program
Swedish American Hospital
1400 Charles Street
Rockford, IL 61108
(815) 966-2273

Central East Alcoholism & Drug
   Council
635 Division
P.O. Box 532
Charleston, IL 61920
(217) 348-8108
Wendy Russell, Director

Chandler & Associates
431 Asbury Avenue
Evanston, IL 60202
(312) 869-1292
Jeanne Chandler

Chicago Dept. of Health
Chicago's Acoholic Treatment Center
3026 S. California Avenue
Chicago, IL 60608
(312) 254-3680
Richard E. Sherman, Ph.D.

Daybreak Program
220 W. Lincoln
Belleville, IL 62220
(618) 235-6532
Gary Pippenger

DePaul Clinic/NW Chicago
1606 Colonial Parkway
Inverness, IL 60067
(312) 991-0188
Dorothea Schneider

Edgewood-Edwardsville
St. Elizabeth Medical Center
1121 University Drive
Edwardsville, IL 62025
(618) 798-3069

Evanston Hospital
2650 Ridge Avenue
Evanston, IL 60201
(312) 492-6465
Dr. John R. Durburg, Dir.

Family Center for Alcohol-Substance
  Abuse
224 W. Judd Street
Woodstock, IL 60098
(815) 337-0030
Lori Nelson, Program Director

Fellowship House, Inc.
110 Lafayette Street
Anna, IL 62906
(618) 833-4456/2194
Mickey Martin Finch

Forest Hospital & Foundation
555 Wilson Lane
Des Plaines, IL 60016
(312) 635-4100
Gail Fisher, Dir.

Good Samaritan Hospital
Daybreak
605 N. 12th Street
Mt. Vernon, IL 62864
(618) 242-1212
Lynn Downen

Great River Recovery Resources
537 Broadway
Quincy, IL 62301
(217) 224-6300
Jerry Aamoth

Habilitative System
Alcohol/Chemical Abuse Division
415 S. Kilpatrick Street
Chicago, IL 60644
(312) 261-2252
Theodora Binion

Ingalls Alcoholism Treatment Center
One Ingalls Drive
Harvey, IL 60426
(312) 333-2300, Ext. 5410
Nancy Cerny, Coordinator of Outreach
  Marketing

Ingalls on Lincoln Highway
4440 W. Lincoln Highway
Matteson, IL 60443
(800) 543-6543
Nancy Cerny, Coordinator of Outreach
  Marketing

Interventions Medical Referral
  Services
1234 S. Michigan Avenue
Suite 100
Chicago, IL 60605
(312) 663-1020
Intake Counselor

Jane Dickman Center
1665 Woodbury
Woodbury, IL 55125
(612) 291-2822
Central Intake

Lovellton Treatment Center
600 Villa
Elgin, IL 60120
(312) 695-0077
Pat Lonhard

Lutheran Social Services
Alcohol/Drug Dependence
4840 West Byron
Chicago, IL 60641
(312) 282-7800
Jeanne Chandler

New Beginnings at Lincoln West
  Medical Center
ADOLESCENT PROGRAM
2544 W. Montrose Avenue
Chicago, IL 60618
(312) 267-2200
Laurel Rubin

New Day Center for Substance Abuse
Hinsdale Hospital
120 N. Oak Street
Hinsdale, IL 60521
(312) 887-2800
Carolyn Grandstaff

New Day Center
Hyde Park Community Hospital
5800 Stoney Island
Chicago, IL 60637
(312) 643-9200
David Budlong

Northwest Youth Outreach
Adolescent Outpatient
6417 W. Irving Park Road
Chicago, IL 60634
(312) 777-7112
William Southwick

Olympia Fields Alcoholism Counseling
  & Family Recovery Program
2440 W. Lincoln Highway
Olympia Fields, IL 60461
(312) 747-3100
Marlene Winter

Parkside Lodge of Mundelein, Inc.
24647 N. Highway 21
Mundelein, IL 60060
(312) 634-2020
Merrill Kempfert

Parkside Youth Center, Inc.
1700 N. Western Avenue
Park Ridge, IL 60068
(312) 696-8313
Steve Twadell
Youth Extended Treatment

Prairie Center
122 W. Hill
Champaign, IL 61820
(217) 356-7562

Proctor Community Hospital
Chemical Dependency Center
5409 N. Knoxville
Peoria, IL 61614
(309) 691-1055
Dennis Pope

Rosecrance Center
1505 N. Alpine Road
Rockford, IL 61107
(815) 399-5351
Philip W. Eaton, Executive Director

St. Mary's Substance Abuse Center
1415 Vermont Street
Quincy, IL 62301-311
(217) 223-1200, Ext. 1600
Tom Staff

INDIANA

Anderson Center of St. Johns Chemical
  Dependency Program
2210 Jackson Street
Anderson, IN 46014
(317) 646-8383
George Horaitis, Director

Cameron Treatment Center
416 E. Maumee Street
Angola, IN 46703
(219) 665-2141
Tim Lickteig

CareUnit Hospital Program
Memorial Hospital of Michigan City
Fifth and Pine Streets
Michigan City, IN 46360
(219) 872-9134

CareUnit Hospital Program
Our Lady Mercy Hospital
U.S. Highway 30
Dyer, IN 46311
(219) 322-6802

Crestview Center of Community
  Hospital, Inc.
2201 Hillcrest Drive
Anderson, IN 46012
(317) 649-8568
Michael Erickson

DePaul Clinic/Terre Haute
788 S. 3rd Street
Terre Haute, IN 47807
(812) 234-2114
Steve Archbold

Fairbanks Hospital
8102 Clearvista Parkway
Indianapolis, IN 46256
(317) 849-8222
Jean Wright, Program Director

Grant-Blackford Mental Health Center
505 Wabash Avenue
Marion, IN 46952
(317) 662-3971
Diane Ashley, R.N., B.S.N.

Grovertown Youth Programs
Substance Abuse
Rural Rt. 1, Box 19
Grovertown, IN 46531
(219) 867-4571

Hamilton Center, Inc.
Alcohol/Drug Services
615 Eighth Avenue
Terre Haute, IN 47804
(812) 231-8323
Dr. C.W. Brett

Ingalls on Ridge Road
900 Ridge Road
Munster, IN 46321
Nancy Cerny, Coordinator of Outreach
  Marketing

Koala Adolescent Center
1404 S. State Avenue
Indianapolis, IN 46203
(317) 783-4084
Barbara Porter

Koala Center
1800 N. Oak Road
P.O. Box 638
Plymouth, IN 46563
(219) 936-3784
Tom Hagan

Koala Outpatient
8925 N. Meridian, Suite 105
Indianapolis, IN 46260
(317) 848-7666
Bonney Awbrey

Koala Outreach
4333 E. Third Street
Bloomington, IN 47401
(812) 333-3012
Howard Clark

Koala Outreach
1415 Vaxter Avenue
Clarksville, IN 47130
(812) 282-7333
Carol Blankenship

Koala Outreach
2824-B 173rd Street
Hammond, IN 46323
(219) 844-7400

Koala Outreach
2957 N. Oakwood Avenue
Muncie, IN 47304
(317) 286-1614
Rita Stoyer

Koala Outreach
Gateway Center Building
425 N. Michigan Street,
Suite 216
South Bend, IN 46601
(219) 282-8592
Jane Reed

Parkside Lodge at Mulberry Center
500 S.E. Fourth Street
Evansville, IN 47713
(812) 426-8201
Patrick Rhoades

Renaissance Center for Addictions
  Services
610 Arcade Avenue
P.O. Box 1329
Elkhart, IN 46515
(219) 522-5522
John Yeager, Director

St. Vincent Stress Center
Chemical Dependency Unit
8401 Harcourt Road
P.O. Box 80160
Indianapolis, IN 46280
(317) 875-4710
Linda Duff

Washington House, Inc.
Detoxification Center
2720 Culbertson Street
Fort Wayne, IN 46804
(219) 432-8684
Thom E. Dyer

IOWA

Alcohol & Drug Dependence Services
  of Southeast Iowa
1340 Mt. Pleasant
Burlington, IA 52601
(319) 753-6567
Art Henriksen

Chemical Dependency Unit
Marian Health Center
2010 Court Street
Sioux City, IA 51102
(712) 279-2480
Mari Kaptain-Dahlan
Program Director

Fountain Center/Eldora
Women's Unit
2413 Edington Avenue
Eldora, IA 50627
(515) 858-5416
Shelley Clingerman

Fountain Center/Forest City
Highway 9 E
Forest City, IA 50436
(515) 582-3113
Michael McGinnis

Gordon Chemical Dependency Center
2700 Pierce Street
2nd Floor, Bldg. E
Sioux City, IA 51104
(712) 258-4578
Judy Carpenter, Adm. Coord.

Mercy's Outpatient Alcoholism
  Recovery Center II
1421 S. Bluff Blvd.
Clinton, IA 52732
(319) 243-7237
Mike Shovlin

Mid-Eastern Council on Chemical
  Abuse
430 Southgate Avenue
Iowa City, IA 52240
(319) 351-4357
Kerry Bartlett,
Treatment Director

Our Primary Purpose
Center for Adolescents
University at Penn
Des Moines, IA 50316
(515) 263-5582
Kathy Maudsley

Powell 3 Treatment Center
Iowa Methodist Medical Center
1200 Pleasant Street
Des Moines, IA 50308
(515) 283-6431
Jean Bartholomew

Sediacek Treatment Center
Mercy Hospital
701 Tenth Street, S.E.
Cedar Rapids, IA 52403
(319) 398-6266
Barbara Martens

The University of Iowa
Chemical Dependency Center
Oakdale Hall
Oakdale, IA 52319
(319) 353-4412
Pat Jensen, Assoc. Dir.

KANSAS

Assessment & Counseling Center
Primary Out Treatment Evenings
7840 Washington Boulevard
Suite 300
Kansas City, KS 66112
(913) 334-6300
C.L. Engebritson

Assessment & Counseling Center
Primary Out Treatment Evenings
9101 W. 110, Suite 234
Overland Park, KS 66210
(913) 451-2610
C.L. Engebritson

CareUnit Hospital Program
Stormont-Vail Regional Medical Center
1500 S.W. 10th Street
Topeka, KS 66606
(913) 354-6797

Central Kansas Foundation for Alcohol
  & Chemical Dependency
903 E. Prescott Street
P.O. Box 2117
Salina, KS 67401
(913) 825-6224
Scott Bogart

DePaul/Kansas
10000 W. 75th Street
Suite 103
Merriam, KS 66204
(913) 384-HOPE
Jim Eiker

Menninger Hospital
Alcohol-Drug Recovery Program
P.O. Box 829
Topeka, KS 66606
(913) 273-7599
Robert Meyers, CAC

Parallax Program, Inc.
520 N. Broadway
Wichita, KS 67214
(316) 267-3395
Milt Fowler

Parkside Lodge of Kansas, Inc.
2100 N. Jackson Avenue
Hutchinson, KS 67501
(316) 663-4800
Glenn Leonardi

Southeast Kansas Mental Health Center
1106 S. 9th, Box 39
Humboldt, KS 66748
(316) 473-2241
Mr. Paul Thomas

St. Francis Hospital & Medical Center
Chemical Dependency Treatment
  Center
1700 W. 7th
Topeka, KS 67218
(800) 432-0976
Don Rees, Director

St. Joseph Medical Center
Alcoholism Treatment Unit
3600 E. Harry
Wichita, KS 67218
(316) 689-4850
David L. Trudeau, M.D.

KENTUCKY

Charter Hospital of Paducah
P.O. Box 7609
Paducah, KY 42001
(502) 444-0444
Judy House, Administrator

Charterton Hospital
Adolescent Unit
704 E. Jefferson Street
LaGrange, KY 40031
(502) 222-0375
Masoud Hejazi, M.D.

Jefferson Alcohol and Drug Abuse
  Center
600 S. Preston Street
Louisville, KY 40202
(502) 583-3951
Diane Hague

Our Lady of Peace Hospital
2020 Newburg Road
Louisville, KY 40232
(502) 451-3330
Bill Emonz, Director of Substance
  Abuse

Regional Alcohol Resource (RAR)
Route 1, Box 418
Henderson KY 42420
(502) 827-2380
Mr. Tomes, Director

LOUISIANA

Alpha Omega Institute of Metairie, Inc.
3108 Cleary, Suite 201
Metairie, LA 70002
(504) 456-9298
Harold Morris

Bowling Green New Orleans
P.O. Box 417
Mandeville, LA 70488
(800) 432-0877
Exec. Dir. (504) 626-5661

Brantley Baptist Center
201 Magazine Street
New Orleans, LA 70130
(504) 523-5761
Dr. T.E. Lilly/Dr. Charles Holmes

CDU of Acadiana
P.O. Box 91526
Lafayette, LA 70509
(318) 234-5614
Ron Weller

CDU of Baton Rouge, Inc.
P.O. Box 4109
4040 N. Boulevard
Baton Rouge, LA 70821
(504) 387-7900
Beryl Smith, Director

Charter Forest Hospital
9320 Linwood Avenue
Shreveport, LA 71106
(318) 688-3930
Mike Womack

Cypress-Alcohol & Drug Program/
  Cypress Adolescent Program
302 Dulles Drive
Lafayette, LA 70506
(318) 233-9024
Julie Simon Dronet, Dir.

F. Edward Herbert, C.D.U.
New Beginnings
1 Sanctuary Drive
New Orleans, LA 70114
(504) 363-2580
Russ Faulkinberry

HCA Cypress Hospital
Alcohol & Drug Program
302 Dulles Drive
Lafayette, LA 70506
(318) 233-9024
Program Director

HCA DePaul Hospital
New Life Center
1040 Calhoun Street
New Orleans, LA 70118
(504) 895-6364
Program Director

HCA Parkland Hospital
Silkworth Center
2414 Bunker Hill Drive
Baton Rouge, LA 70808
(504) 927-9050
Service Director

Koala Center at Opelousas
General Hospital
520 Prudhomme Lane
Opelousas, LA 70570
(318) 948-8070
Fred Hill

MAINE

The Alcohol Institute
Mercy Hospital
144 State Street
Portland, ME 04101
(207) 879-3346
Betsy Turner

Down East Community Hospital
  Substance Abuse Treatment
  Program
Route 1, Box 11
Machias, ME 04654
(207) 255-3356
Dru Myers, Director

Merrymeeting Treatment
  Center—Alcohol & Chemical
  Dependence
51 Center Road
Bowdeinham, ME 04008
(207) 666-5583
Patricia Conner, Director Alc. Services

St. Mary's General
Chemical Unit
45 Golden Street
Lewiston, ME 04240
(207) 786-2901
(800) 442-9858
George K. Dreher

Westbrook Community Hospital
Chemical Dependency Program
40 Park Road
Westbrook, ME 04092
(207) 854-8464
Paul Rannuci or Nursing Department

York County Counseling Services
333 Lincoln Street
P.O. Box 1010
Saco, ME 04072
(207) 282-7504
Dr. Thomas Kane, Executive Director

MARYLAND

Greater Baltimore Medical Center
6701 N. Charles Street
Baltimore, MD 21204
(301) 828-2301
Joseph S. Lemmon

Oakview Treatment Center
3100 Health Park Drive
Ellicott City, MD 21043
(301) 461-9922
Bob Witt

Psychiatric Institute of Montgomery
  County
14901 Broschart Road
Rockville, MD 20850
(301) 251-4545
Dr. Jodie Smith

The Resource Group
7402 York Road, Suite 101
Baltimore, MD 21204
(301) 337-7772
Gloria B. Uhl

The Sheppard & Enoch Pratt Hospital,
  Inc.
P.O. Box 6815
Towson, MD 21204
(301) 823-8200
Dr. David Walter, Dir. of Admissions

MASSACHUSETTS

Adult Children Counseling Center at
 LifeCycle
114 Farlow Road
Newton MA 02158
(617) 244-2792

Berkshire Council on Alcoholism
214 Francis Avenue
Pittsfield, MA 01201
(413) 499-9000
Kate Angelni

Doyle Detox
793 North Street
Pittsfield, MA 01201
(413) 499-0337
Rosemary Wetherell

Gay & Lesbian Counseling Service
Substance Abuse Program
600 Washington Street
Suite 652
Boston, MA 02111
(617) 542-5188
Nancy Grantham, Director
Hot Line (617) 426-9371
Monday-Friday 6 PM - 11 PM

Gosnold Treatment
200 Ter Heun Drive
Falmouth, MA 02540
(617) 540-6550
Rav Tamasi

High Point Alcoholism Treatment
 Facility/Mass
1233 State Road
(Route 3A)
Plymouth, MA 02345
(617) 224-7701
Dr. Edward T. Less

New Day Center
Fuller Memorial Hospital
231 Washington Street
South Attleboro, MA 02703
(617) 761-8500
Bill White

The Norcap Center at Southwood
 Community Hospital
111 Dedham Street
Norfolk, MA 02056
(617) 668-0385, Ext. 360
Leroy Kelly

Whitmans Pond
Family Services
210 Winter Street
Suite 204
Weymouth, MA 02188
(617) 331-6320
Rachel Figa

MICHIGAN

Bay Haven Chemical Dependency
 Program
Samaritan Health Center
713 9th Street
Bay City, MI 48708
(517) 894-3799
Admission Counselor

Bixby Hospital Sage Center—Alcohol
 & Substance Abuse
818 Riverside Avenue
Adrian, MI 49221
(517) 263-0711, Ext. 411
Edward Skinner, M.A., C.S.W.

CareUnit of Grand Rapids
1931 Boston, S.E.
Grand Rapids, MI 48603
(616) 243-2273

The Caring Centers
4709 State Street
Saginaw, MI 48603
(517) 790-3366
Clinical Supervisor

Catherine McAuley Health
   Center—Chemical Dependency
   Program
P.O. Box 2506
Ann Arbor, MI 48106
(313) 572-4303
Neil Carolan

Chemical Dependency Resources
1407 Comerica Building
Battle Creek, MI 49017
(616) 968-2811
Jeffrey N. Andert, Ph.D

Eastwood Clinics
Corporate Office
15085 E. Seven Mile
Detroit, MI 48205
(313) 526-6000

Farmington Area Advisory
   Council—Outpatient Substance
   Abuse Program
23450 Middlebelt Road
Farmington Hills, MI 48024
(313) 477-6767
Betty Arnold

Glenbeigh of Kent
Community Hospital
750 Fuller Avenue, N.E.
Grand Rapids, MI 49503
(616) 242-6550
Richard Coggins

Harold E. Fox Center
Substance Abuse Programs
St. Joseph Mercy Hospital
900 Woodward Avenue
Pontiac, MI 48053
(313) 858-3177
Robert Kercorian

Henry Ford Hospital
Maplegrove Centers
6773 W. Maple Road
West Bloomfield, MI 48033
(313) 661-6100
Admissions Office

Highland Waterford Center
Outpatient
377 S. Telegraph Road
Pontiac, MI 48053
(313) 338-6616
Dennis Angrisani

Holly Gardens Detox Residential
   Program
4501 Grange Hall Road
Holly, MI 48442
(313) 634-0140
Bill Epling

Industrial Rehabilitation Center,
   A Koala Center
1207 N. Ballenger
Flint, MI 48504
(313) 767-1190
Bill Trosko

Insight at Botsford
General Hospital
28050 Grand River
Farmington Hills, MI 48024
(313) 471-8583
Dan Chambers

Insight at Flint
Osteopathic Hospital
3921 Beecher Road
Flint, MI 48504
(313) 762-4627
Charles McPhail

Insight at Hurley
Medical Center
One Hurley Plaza
Flint, MI 48502
(313) 257-9412
John McKellar

Insight at Riverside
Osteopathic Hospital
150 Traux Street
Trenton, MI 48183
(313) 676-4200
Jim Stone

Insight at Saginaw
General Hospital
1447 N. Harrison
Saginaw, MI 48602
(517) 771-4298
Steve Johnson

Insight Intensive
Outpatient Program
The White House
Professional Center
G-3255 Beecher Road
Flint, MI 48504
(313) 733-3988
Dawn Ferran

Insight Outpatient Clinic
Leemen Centre
2241 S. Linden Road
Flint, MI 48504
(313) 733-0900
Jackie Loiselle

Marquette General Hospital
Substance Abuse Services
420 W. Magnetic Street
Marquette, MI 49855
(906) 225-3330
Patricia Tikkanen

Munson Medical Center
Alcoholism/Drug Dependency
   Program
Sixth & Madison Streets
Traverse City, MI 49684
(616) 922-9238
Charles Bethea

New Day Center—Battle Creek
   Adventist Hospital
165 N. Washington Avenue
Battle Creek, MI 49016
(616) 964-7121
John Jozwiak

New Day Center—Tri-County
   Community Hospital
1131 E. Howard City/Edmore Road
Edmore, MI 48829
(517) 427-5116
Steve Guthrie

Ottagan Alcoholic Rehabilitation
118 E. 9th Street
Holland, MI 49423
(616) 396-5284
Ralph Edgington

The Oxford Institute
Chemical Dependency
825 W. Drahner Road
P.O. Box 429
Oxford, MI 48051
(313) 628-0500
Virginia Biegun

Riverview Center
18591 Quarry Road
Riverview, MI 48192
(313) 282-2626
Connie Clem, Program Director

Sage Center for Substance Abuse
   Treatment/Bixby Hospital
818 Riverside Avenue
Adrian, MI 49221
(517) 263-0711, Ext. 411
Edward Skinner, Program Director

St. Lawrence Hospital
Addictions Programs
4000 N. Michigan Road
Dimondale, MI 48821
(517) 646-6622
Terry Hagan

Washtenaw Council on Alcoholism
2301 Platt Road
Ann Arbor, MI 48104
(363) 971-7900
Barry K. Kistner

Woodland Hills
755 W. Big Beaver, Suite 2009
Troy, MI 48084
(313) 362-2610
Dr. Harvey Halberstadt

MINNESOTA

Abbott North Western
Willow Street Center
1375 Willow Street
Minneapolis, MN 55403
(612) 879-1100
Nancy Cox

ARC Parkview
3705 Park Center Boulevard
Minneapolis, MN 55416
(612) 929-5531
Normandy Hamilton

CareUnit Hospital Program
Golden Valley Health Center
4101 Golden Valley Road
Golden Valley, MN 55442
(612) 588-2771

Central Mesabi Treatment Center
750 E. 34th Street
Hibbing, MN 55746
(218) 262-5587
Wes Halvorson

Fairview Deaconess Hospital
Adolescent Chemical Dependency
   Program
1400 E. 24th Street
Minneapolis, MN 55404
(612) 721-9334 / 721-9338
Gregg Larson, Admin. Sup.

Fountain Center
Adolescent Treatment Unit
408 Fountain Street
Albert Lea, MN 56007
(507) 373-2384
Joyce Mullenmaster

Fountain Center/Albert Lea
408 Fountain Street
Albert Lea, MN 56007
(507) 373-2384
Darrell Aldrich

Fountain Center/Winnebago
Winnebago Adolescent Unit
550 Cleveland Avenue W.
Winnebago, MN 56098
(507) 893-4848
J. Curtis Murphy

Hazelden-Lakeview
700 Cedar Street,
Suite 127
Alexandria, MN 56308
(612) 762-8135
Jerry Currier

Hazelden Pioneer House
11505 36th Avenue North
Plymouth, MN 55441
(612) 559-2022
Mike Schicks

Hazelden Rehabilitation
Box 11
Center City, MN 55012
(612) 257-4010
Wayne Brandenburg

The Irene Whitney Center for
   Recovery
4954 Upton Avenue South
Minneapolis, MN 55410
(612) 922-3825
Betty Grilliegi/Bonnie Ployhar

Jamestown
11559 Jasmine Trail N.
Stillwater, MN 55082
(612) 429-5307
Jack T. Vigen

Louis House North
Substance Abuse Program
1000 Paul Parkway
Blaine, MN 55434
(612) 757-2906
David Rosenker

Louis House Treatment
   Center—Adolescent Treatment
   Program
115 Forestview Lane North
Plymouth, MN 55441
(612) 546-8008
Sharlee Benson

Minnesota Indian Primary
   Residence—Substance Abuse
   Treatment Center
P.O. Box 66
Sawyer, MN 55780
(218) 879-6731
Elwin Benton

Minnesota Institute on Black Chemical
   Abuse
2616 Nicollet Avenue South
Minneapolis, MN 55408
(612) 871-7878
Peter Bell/Boissan Moore

New Beginnings Recovery Center of
   America Inc.
Outpatient Program
7325 Wayzata Boulevard
Minneapolis, MN 55426
(612) 540-0128
Bill Wingreene

New Visions Treatment
   Center—Substance Abuse Programs
2605 2nd Avenue S.
Minneapolis, MN 55408
(612) 870-0441
Terry Smith
Serving Primarily
American Indian Clientele

On-Belay Halfway House for
   Chemically Dependent Adolescents
1502 Archwood Road
Minnetonka, MN 55343
(612) 544-2097
Lori Boquist

Primary Mental Health Care
LIFE DESIGN
7750 France Avenue S.
Suite 210
Minneapolis, MN 55435
(612) 831-6516
Mr. Robert Subby, M.A., C.C.D.P.

Renaissance, Inc.
2445 Winnetka Avenue N.
Golden Valley, MN 55427
(612) 544-2525
Jerry Burg, Exec. Dir.

Sherburne Extended Care
550 Caltier Street
St. Paul, MN 55103
(612) 227-5515
Myrna Hrubetz

St. Mary's Chemical Dependency
   Services
2512 S. Seventh Street
Minneapolis, MN 55454
(612) 338-2234
(800) 231-2234 (Out of MN)
Mary Houff, Ext. 481

Team Center
54 W. Exchange Street
St. Paul, MN 55102
(612) 291-2822
Central Intake

Triumph Life Center
555 Simpson Street
St. Paul, MN 55104
(612) 642-9363
Out of MN (800) 342-8722
Carl Eller

2020 Adolescent Receiving
2020 Minnehaha Avenue S.
Minneapolis, MN 55404
(612) 371-6953
Supervisor

Twin Town Treatment
1706 University Avenue
St. Paul, MN 55104
(800) 645-3662
Chuck Daley, Director

Warren Eustis Center
720 O'Neal Drive
Eagan, MN 55121
(612) 291-2822
Central Intake

Way Halfway Chemical Dependency
   Psychiatric Component
645 E. Wayzata Boulevard
Wayzata, MN 55391
(612) 473-7371

MISSISSIPPI

Mississippi Baptist Medical Center
   CDC
1225 N. State Street
Jackson, MS 39201
(601) 968-1102
Mary Ross

Mississippi State Hospital
Alcohol Treatment Center
Whitfield
Whitfield, MS 39193
(601) 939-1221, Ext. 236
Dr. Jim Service, Director

MISSOURI

CareUnit Hospital of St. Louis
1755 Grand Boulevard
St. Louis, MO 63104
(314) 771-0500

CareUnit Hospital Program
Baptist Medical Center
6601 Rockhill Road
Kansas City, MO 64131
(816) 361-8020

Christin Hospital
Recovery Center
1225 Graham Road
Florissant, MO 63031
(314) 839-1250
Nancy Snow, Admin. Dir.

The Edgewood Program
St. John's Mercy Medical Center
615 S. New Ballas Road
St. Louis, MO 63141
(314) 569-6500
Lyle Cameron, Director

HCA Research Psychiatric
   Center—Substance Abuse Program
2323 E. 63rd Street
Kansas City, MO 64130
(816) 444-8161
Program Manager

Koala Center
Maupin Road & Highway FF,
P.O. Box 90
Londell, MO 63060
(314) 629-5100
Mike Gardine

Lindell Hospital Comprehensive
  Treatment Unit
4930 Lindell
St. Louis, MO 63108
(314) 367-3770
Robert L. Williams, Ph.D.

New Beginnings at Laughlin Pavillion
900 E. LaHarpe
Kirksville, MO 63501
(816) 665-3713
Bill Booth/Donna Peissner
Adult & Adolescent Programs

St. Charles Program
St. Joseph Health Center
300 First Capitol Drive
St. Charles, MO 63301
(314) 947-5140
Tim Carl

St. Joseph's Hospital
Family Recovery Program
525 Couch Avenue
Kirkwood, MO 63022
(314) 966-1500
Jack O'Keefe

Southeast Missouri Community
  Treatment Center—Aquinas
P.O. Drawer 459
Farmington, MO 63640
(314) 756-5749
Barron E. Pratte, Ph.D.

MONTANA

F M Deaconess Hospital
Chemical Dependency Center
621 3rd Street South
Glasgow, MT 59230
(800) 422-5683
(406) 228-2776
Dave Brunelle

Hill-Top Recovery, Inc.
Chemical Dependency Treatment
  Center
P.O. Box 750
1020 Assiniboine
Havre, MT 59501
(406) 265-9665

Recovery Northwest
Substance Abuse Programs
P.O. Box 756
Libby, MT 59923
(406) 293-7731
Dennis Maercklein,
Program Director

Rimrock Foundation
1231 N. 29th
Billings, MT 59101
(406) 248-3175
David Cunningham,
Executive Director

Shodair Adolescent Chemical
  Dependency Unit
840 Helena Avenue
P.O. Box 5539
Helena, MT 59604
(406) 442-1980
Douglas Settles, Dir.

NEBRASKA

Eppley Treatment Center
3512 Cuming Street
Omaha, NE 68131
(402) 397-3150, Ext. 521
Christopher Eiel, Dir.

Immanuel Alcoholism Treatment
  Center
6901 N. 72nd Street
Omaha, NE 68122
(402) 572-2016
Jim Mays

Lincoln General Hospital
Independence Center
2440 St. Mary's Avenue
Lincoln, NE 68502
(402) 473-5268
Ron Namuth

Santa Monica, Inc.
Transitional
130 N. 39th Street
Omaha, ME 68131
(402) 558-7088
Nelle Linder

South Omaha Alcoholism Outpatient
  Counseling Agency
5211 S. 31st Street
Omaha, NE 68107
(402) 734-3000
Marjorie Wise

Youth Treatment Center
Lincoln General Hospital
2419 St. Mary's Avenue
Lincoln, NE 68502
(402) 473-5394
Malcolm Heard

NEVADA

CareUnit Hospital of Nevada
5100 West Sahara
Las Vegas, NV 89102
(702) 362-8404

HCA The Montevista Centre
Substance Abuse Unit
5900 W. Rochelle Avenue
Las Vegas, NV 89103
(702) 364-1111
Program Manager

HCA Truckee Meadows Hospital
  North—Alcohol & Substance Abuse
  Treatment Program
2100 El Rancho Drive
Sparks, NV 89431
(702) 323-0478
Program Director

New Frontier Treatment Center
165 N. Carson Street
Fallon, NV 89406
(702) 423-6048
Kevin Quint

Tri-County Counseling Service—
  Alcohol/Substance Abuse Programs
1802 N. Carson Street
Suite 210
Carson City, NV 89701
(702) 883-2720
Jerry Nolan

Vitality Center
3740 E. Idaho Street
Elko, NV 89801
(702) 738-8004
Peter Goeser,
Treatment Coordinator

NEW HAMPSHIRE

Beech Hill Hospital, Inc.
Dublin, NH 03444
(603) 563-8511
John H. Valentine, President

Hampstead Hospital
East Road
Hampstead, NH 03878
(603) 329-5311
Allan Carney, Prgm. Dir.

Southeastern New Hampshire Services
50 Chestnut Street
Box 978
Dover, NH 03820
(603) 749-3981
Mr. J. Green/Mr. W. Kohut

Spofford Hall
P.O. Box 225
Spofford, NH 03262
(603) 363-4545

NEW JERSEY

Camden County Alcohol Abuse
  Program
2101 Ferry Avenue, Suite 204
Camden, NJ 01804
(609) 757-3481
Mary Ann Clayton, Director

Endeavor House
Halfway House for Men
6 Broadway
Keyport, NJ 07735
(201) 264-3824
Zee Rocker, Director

Fair Oaks Hospital
Substance Abuse Treatment
19 Prospect Street
Summit, NJ 07901
(800) 526-4494
(201) 522-7000
Admissions

The Harbor Alcoholism
Treatment Center
1405 Clifton Street
Hoboken, NJ 07030
(201) 656-4040
Program Director

Kids of Bergen County, Inc.
P.O. Box 4407
River Edge, NJ 07661
(201) 487-4100
Pat Hagan, Intake Coord.

Maryville Alcohol Rehab.
  Center—Outpatient Division
  (Inpatient Refer)
645 N. Broad Street
Woodbury, NJ 08096
(609) 845-3647
(609) 881-6400
Jerry Washko

Monmouth Chemical Dependency
  Treatment Center
152 Chelsea Avenue
Long Branch, NJ 07740
(201) 222-5190
William R. Stender

New Beginnings at Lakehurst
440 Beckerville Road
Lakehurst, NJ 08733
(201) 657-4800
Charles Ward
Executive Director

Seabrook House
P.O. Box 5055, Polk Lane
Seabrook, NJ 08302-0655
(609) 455-7575
Charles Reinert

St. Clare's Riverside Medical Center
Powerville Road
Boonton, NJ 07005
(201) 334-5000
Clark MacWright

Van Ost Institute for Family Living, Inc.
113 Engle Street
Englewood, NJ 07631
(201) 569-6667
Judy Pool, Prog. Dir.

NEW MEXICO

Alamo Alcoholism Program
Outpatient
P.O. Box 488
Alamo, NM 87825
(505) 854-2543 or
(505) 854-2626
June Mexicano

CareUnit Hospital of Albuquerque
505 High Street N.E.
Albuquerque, NM 87102
(505) 848-8088

Four Winds Alcoholism
Rehabilitation Center
P.O. Box 736
Farmington, NM 87499
(505) 327-7218
Orlando Piache

HCA Heights Psychiatric Hospital
  Alcohol/Substance Abuse Treatment
  Program
103 Hospital Loop, N.E.
Albuquerque, NM 87109
(505) 883-8777
Admissions Coordinator

New Beginnings at Amethyst Hall
6930 Weicker Lane
P.O. Box 160
Velards, NM 87582
(505) 852-2704
Ron Shepphard

The Resource Center
Substance Abuse Program
1039 A. High Street
P.O. Drawer 966
Grants, NM 87020
(505) 287-7985
Michael Johnson

Thoreau Alcoholism Program, Inc.
Second & Olive
Thoreau, NM 87233
(505) 862-7580
Lynda Pratt

NEW YORK

A.C.T.
211 W. 56th Street
Suite 30M
New York, NY 10019
(212) 362-4042
(212) 315-3449
Sephanie Kravec, C.S.W.

Alive and Well
900 Walt Whitman Road
Melville, NY 11747
(516) 423-3955
Ken Helton

Arms Acres
P.O. Box X
Carmel, NY 10512
(914) 225-3400

Areba-Casriel Institute
500 W. 57th Street
New York, NY 10019
(212) 247-4920
Steven J. Yohay

Benjamin Rush Center
Chemical Abuse Recovery Service
672 South Salina Street
Syracuse, NY 13202
(315) 476-2161
In NY (800) 647-6479
Admissions
Outpatient Services
Stan Long (315) 476-2185

Bry-Lin Hospital, Inc.
Rush Hall
1263 Delaware Avenue
Buffalo, NY 14209
(716) 886-8200
Robert J. Bertone
Michael C. Welsh

Conifer Park
Alcohol/Drug Programs
150 Glenridge Road
Scotia, NY 12302
(518) 399-6446
Gail Harkness

Ellis Hospital Alcoholism Day & Night
   Program
1101 Nott Street
Schenectady, NY 12308
(518) 382-4179
Marty Wakesburg

Four Winds Hospital
800 Cross River Road
Katonah, NY 10536
(914) 763-8151
Diane Biumi
Director of Admissions

Four Winds—Saratoga
30 Crescent Avenue
Saratoga Springs, NY 12866
(518) 584-3600
Brenda Quinn, N.S.W.
Director of Admissions

Freeport Medical Associates
P.C. Consultation Center
224 W. 35th Street, Suite 1401
New York, NY 10001
(212) 279-2727
Walter Scanlon, Director

Livingston County Council on
   Alcoholism Treatment
(Drink/Drive Program)
Livingston Campus, Bldg. #2
Mt. Morris, NY 14510
(716) 658-2216
Robert Greenberg or Secretary

The Lowell Institute
535 Fifth Avenue
New York, NY 10017
(212) 661-1740
Tom Sleavin, M.P.A.

Park Ridge
Chemical Dependency
1565 Long Pond Road
Rochester, NY 14626
(716) 227-6505
James M. Damon

St. Luke's—Roosevelt Hospital Center
Comprehensive Treatment Program
324 W. 108th Street
New York, NY 10025
(212) 678-6315
Dr. Gail Allen
Donald Jordan, Admin.

South Oaks Hospital
400 Sunrise Highway
Amityville, NY 11701
(516) 264-4000
Leonard W. Krinsky, Ph.D.

St. Peter's Hospital
Alcoholism Rehabilitation Center
315 S. Manning Blvd.
Albany, NY 12208
(518) 454-1301
Karen A. Bondi

St. Vincent's
Bayley Seton Hospital
297 Bard Avenue
Staten Island, NY 10310
(718) 390-1445
Carol Ahrens

Veritas Villa
RR 2, Box 415
Krehonkson, NY 12446
(914) 626-3555
Jack McGonigle

The Weekend Center for Treatment of
    Alcohol Related Problems
359 Main Street
Mt. Kisco, NY 10549
(914) 666-6740
Adrienne Marcus

W.J. Finnegan Associates
Family Psychotherapists
91 Union Avenue
Saratoga Springs, NY 23866
(518) 587-9298
(518) 587-7961
Walter J. Finnegan, CEO

NORTH CAROLINA

Bridgeway A Chaps
Treatment Program
Hospital Drive,
P.O. Box 1116
Brevard, NC 28712
(704) 884-2100
Dorothy Worley, Program Director

CareUnit Hospital Program
Alamance County Hospital
327 N. Graham-Hopedale Road
Burlington, NC 27215
(919) 226-4382

Carolina Manor Treatment Center of
    Lumberton
1100 Pine Run Drive
Lumberton, NC 28358
(919) 738-1191
Morris Barbour

Charlotte Treatment Center
P.O. Box 240197
1715 Sharon Road W.
Charlotte, NC 28224
(704) 554-8373
James F. Emmert, Director

Hopewell
P.O. Box 1101
Asheville, NC 28802
(704) 254-3201
Richard Selman, M.D.

New Day Center of Park Ridge Hospital
1801 Asheville Highway
Hendersonville, NC 28732
(704) 693-6224
Steve Gambrel

Orange Person Chatham
Mental Health Center
333 McMasters Street
Chapel Hill, NC 27514
(919) 929-0471
Tim Slaven, Substance Abuse Director

Pinehurst Treatment Center
A Chaps Treatment Program
Box 3000
Pinehurst, NC 28374
(919) 295-7902
Bill Sitnik, Program Director

The Randolph Clinic, Inc.
100 Billingsley Road
Charlotte, NC 28211
(704) 376-2431
Henry T. Finch, Jr.

Wake County Alcoholism Treatment
    Center
3000 Falstaff Road
Raleigh, NC 27610
(919) 821-7650
Judy Gooding

Woodhill Drug Alcohol Treatment
  Center
Caledonia Road
P.O. Box 5534
Asheville, NC 28813
(704) 253-3681
(800) 438-4871
Dennis Moore, Pharm Dir.

NORTH DAKOTA

Badlands Human Service Center
Drug & Alcohol Services
Pulver Hall
Dickenson, ND 58601
(701) 227-2771, Ext. 68
Edward Sheaa

Council on Alcohol & Drug Problems,
  Inc.
1201 13th Avenue S
Grand Forks, ND 58201
(701) 772-7203
John Hennessy, MAC

Crossroads Center of St. John's
  Hospital
510 S. 4th Street
Fargo, ND 58103
(701) 232-3331
John J. Allen, Dir.
Outpatient programs:
Mayville 786-3800
Valley City 845-0440

Heartview Foundation
1406 2nd Street, N.W.
Mandan, ND 48554
(701) 663-2321
Dr. Mark Hanlon

United Recovery Center
Medical Park
Grand Forks, ND 58206
Jim Luse

OHIO

Adolescent Chemical Dependency
  Program
11311 Shaker Boulevard
Cleveland, OH 44104
(216) 368-7970
Clayton R. Moschetti-Houff

Alcohol/Drug Dependency Services,
  Inc. (ADDS Inc.)
246 Northland Drive
Medina, OH 44256
(216) 723-3641
Gail Ritchie, Director

Bethesda Alcohol & Drug Treatment
  Programs
619 Oak Street
Cincinnati, OH 45206
(513) 569-6014
Mark Davis
Adolescent Day Treatment
Program (513) 530-0050

The Campus Alcoholism
Services for Young Adults
905 S. Sunbury Road
Westerville, OH 43081
(614) 895-1000
Michael Thomson
Program Director

CareUnit Hospital of Cincinnati
3156 Glenmore Avenue
Cincinnati, OH 45211
(513) 481-8822

CareUnit Hospital Program
Community MedCenter Hospital
1050 Delaware Avenue
Marion, OH 43302
(614) 387-6408

The Center Drug & Alcohol Program
91 Park Avenue W.
Mansfield, OH 44902
(419) 525-1144
Anne Sabri

Edwin Shaw Hospital
1621 Flickinger Road
Akron, OH 44312
(216) 784-1271
Robin Louis

First City Recovery Center, Inc.
427 Second Street
Marietta, OH 45750
(614) 373-0654
Markorie A. Kimmel, CAC

Flower Memorial Hospital
Chemical Dependency Center
5200 Harroun Road
Sylvania, OH 43560
(419) 885-1444, Ext. 4571
Cynthia Krause, Program Director

Freedom Hall Alcohol Chemical
   Dependency Programs
291 Heiser Court
Crestline, OH 44827
(419) 683-1212, Ext. 41
Susan Hartzband

Glenbeigh Hospital/Cleveland
18120 Puritas Avenue
Cleveland, OH 44135
(216) 476-0222
Theodore Sucher

Greene Hall
1141 N. Monroe Drive
Xenis, OH 45385
(513) 376-6721
Larry Gault, Director

Interval Brotherhood Home
Alcohol Rehabilitation, Inc.
3445 South Main Street
Akron, OH 44319
(216) 644-4095
Fr. Samuel R. Ciccolini

Lakeland Institute
3500 Kolbe Road
Lorain, OH 44053
(216) 282-7106
Thomas Stuber

Lakeland Institute
6929 W. 130th Street
Parma Heights, OH 44130
(216) 845-7780
Dana Harlow

Lakeland Institute
1801 E. Perkins Street
Sandusky, OH 44870
(419) 625-7106
Charles Dials

Maryhaven
1744 Alum Creek Drive
Columbus, OH 43207
(614) 445-8131
Jack Butler

Merrick Hall Adolescent Chemical
   Dependency Unit
Huron Road Hospital
13951 Terrace Road
Cleveland, OH 44112
(216) 761-2851
Mary Reed

Merrick Hall for Women and
   Adolescents—Mary Reed
13951 Terrace Road
Cleveland, OH 44112
(216) 761-2955
Ms. Linda Roberts

The Oaks Rehabilitative Services
   Center
628 E. Creek
P.O. Box 1404
McAlester, OH 74502
(918) 423-6030
Penny Watson

Saint Luke's Hospital
Adolescent Chemical Dependency
  Program
11311 Shaker Boulevard
Cleveland, OH 44104
(216) 368-7970
Clayton R. Moschetti-Houff, Adm.
  Director

Samaritan Hall Chemical Dependency
  Treatment
4780 Salem Avenue
Dayton, OH 45416
(513) 276-5031
Michael Neatherton, Director

Serenity Hall
Richland Hospital
P.O. Box 637
Mansfield, OH 44901
(800) 221-HOPE
Jerry Seaman

Straight Talk, Inc.
3930 Fulton Drive N.W.
Canton, OH 44718
(216) 493-3064
Beth L. Phillips

Talbot Hall
St. Anthony Medical Center
1492 E. Broad Street
Columbus, OH 43205
(614) 251-3760
Richard R. Schnurr

Tennyson Center
St. Vincent Medical Center
2465 Collingwood Boulevard
Toledo, OH 43620
(419) 255-5665
Margo W. Johnson, M.A.

The Toledo Hospital
Alcoholism Treatment Center
2142 N. Cove Boulevard
Toledo, OH 43606
(419) 241-3662
William Shanahan, Ph.D.

OKLAHOMA

Affiliated Assessment
Guidance Center
800 Rock Creek Road
Suite 109
Norman, OK 73069
(800) 251-0026 US
In KS (800) 432-0678
(405) 329-4816

CareUnit Hospital Program
Hillcrest Medical Center
Utica on the Park
Tulsa, OK 74104
(918) 560-5712

Enid Memorial Hospital
CareUnit
402 S. 4th
Enid, OK 71701
(405) 242-7713
Charla Rasmussen

Greenleaf Center, Inc.
Substance Abuse Program
1601 Gordon Cooper Drive
Shawnee, OK 74801
(405) 275-9610
In OK (800) 654-6454
Betty Mosher

Presbyterian Adolescent Chemical
  Dependency Center
707 N.W. 6th Street
Oklahoma City, OK 73102
(405) 232-0777
Rick Lair Robinson
Family Therapy Required

Shadow Mountain Institute
6262 S. Sheridan
Tulsa, OK 74133
(918) 492-8200
Phil Cottrell

St. Johns Adolescent Chemical
    Dependency Unit
Comanche Memorial Hospital
3401 W. Gore Boulevard
Lawton, OK 73505
(405) 355-8620

St. John's Chemical Dependency
    Treatment Center
6125 W. Reno
Suite 400
Oklahoma City, OK 73127
(405) 495-3080

OREGON

Adapt
P.O. Box 1121
Roseburg, OR 97470
(503) 672-2691
Bruce Piper

B & J Counseling Center
Substance Abuse Programs
2550 Coral Avenue N.E.
Salem, OR 97305
(503) 363-2021
Robert Varner

CareUnit Hospital of Portland
1927 N.W. Lovejoy Street
Portland, OR 97029
(503) 225-0031

DePaul Center, Inc.
1320 S.W. Washington
Portland, OR 97205
(503) 223-4922
James W. Thornton
Daniel M. Dickinson

Mount Hood Medical Center
Alcoholism Treatment Services
24800 S.E. Stark Street,
P.O. Box 718
Gresham, OR 97030
(503) 661-9204
Dr. Gary E. Braden, Director

New Day Center
Portland Adventist Medical
6012 S.E. Yamhill
Portland, OR 97215
(503) 231-3995
Craig Montgomery

Program 180
2800 Barnett Road
Medford, OR 97504
(503) 772-1311
Leslie Koralek

Serenity By The Sea
Chemical Dependency Treatment
    Center
321 S. Prom
Seaside, OR 97138
(800) 452-HELP
Marsha Morgan, Ph.D.

Serenity Lane Chemical Addiction
    Programs
616 E. 16th Avenue
Eugene, OR 97401
(503) 687-1110
Lois O'Connor
Also serving Portland,
Salem & Medford, OR

PENNSYLVANIA

Achates Mental Health Services
7805 McKnight Road
Suite 103
Pittsburgh, PA 15237
(412) 367-4514
Joseph A. Pauza

ARC The Terraces
1170 South State Street
Ephrata, PA 17522
(717) 627-0790
or NE (800) 441-7345

Bowling Green Inn/Brandywine
495 Newark Road
Kennett Square, PA 19348
(215) 268-3588
Community Relations Department

The Bridge Therapeutic Center at Fox
   Chase
8400 Pine Road
Philadelphia, PA 19111
(215) 342-5000
Tracie Kelly

CareUnit Hospital Program
Hamot Medical Center
201 State Street
Erie, PA 16550
(814) 870-6133

Clear Brook Inc.
RD #10 E. Northampton St.
Wilkes-Barre, PA 18702
(717) 823-1171
Dave Lombard, President

Columbia Hospital
Substance Abuse Help Unit
7th & Poplar Street
Columbia, PA 17512
(717) 684-2841
Joe Pritchard

Community Counseling of Union/
   Snyder Counties
27 N. Fifth Street
Lewisburg, PA 17837
(717) 523-3216
Wilbur Peachey, Director

Endless Mountains Treatment Center
520 Ruah Street
Blossburg, PA 16912
(717) 638-2948
Deborah Browning

Eugenia Hospital
ADAPT Programs
660 Thomas Road
Lafayette Hill, PA 19444
(215) 836-1380
Paul F. Peltier

The Fairmount Institute
561 Fairthorne Avenue
Philadelphia, PA 19128
(215) 487-4000
Frank Walls, Program Director

Livengrin Foundation
Alcoholism Treatment
4833 Hulmerville Road
Bensalem, PA 19020
(215) 639-2300
Carl Illenberger

Mirmont Adolescent Family Adult
   Programs
100 Yearsley Mill Road
Lima, PA 19037
(215) 565-9232
Thomas F. Crane

New Beginnings at Cove Forge
P.O. Box B
Route 1, Box 79
Williamsburg, PA 16693
(814) 832-2131
Coni Hilling

Philadelphia Psychiatric Cener
Ford Road & Monument Avenue
Philadelphia, PA 19131
(215) 581-5481
Martha Newbourne

Roxbury—Westcare, Inc.
Drug & Alcohol Rehabilitation
601 Roxbury Road
Shippensburg, PA 17257
(717) 532-4217
Claire F. Beckwith

St. Francis Medical Center
Chemical Dependence
45th Street (off Pennsylvania Avenue)
Pittsburgh, PA 15201
(412) 622-4511
Mr. Michael Flaberty

White Deer Treatment Center (A Koala
    Center)
Devitts Camp Road
P.O. Box 97
Allenwood, PA 17810-0097
(717) 538-2567
Neil Murphey

RHODE ISLAND

Alcoholism Treatment
    Services—Butler Hospital
345 Blackstone Boulevard
Providence, RI 02906
(401) 456-3885
Edward B. Fink, M.D.

Evening Clinic for Alcohol Affected
    Families
4601 Post Road
East Greenwich, RI 02818
(401) 884-1002
Ann Waring

Franek Clinic
4601 Post Road
East Greenwich, RI 02818
(401) 884-1002
E. Ann Waring, Office Mgr.
An Affiliate of Edgehill Newport

The Providence Center
Alcohol Services
520 Hope Street
Providence, RI 02906
(401) 274-2500
Donald Labonte, M.A., C.A.C.

SOUTH CAROLINA

Bruce Hall Center for Treatment of
    Chemical Dependency
121 E. Cedar Street
Florence, SC 29501
(803) 664-3240
Jim Holder

Chaps Baker Treatment Center
2750 Speissegger Drive
North Charleston, SC 29405
(803) 744-2110, Ext. 2931
C.W. Pepper Phillips, Program
    Director

Chaps Columbia Recovery Programs
828 Woodrow Street, Box 50685
Columbia, SC 29250
(803) 771-4414

Charleston Co.—Substance Abuse
    Commission
25 Courtenay Drive
Charleston, SC 29403
(803) 723-7212
Franklin L. Johnson, Executive
    Director

Charter Rivers Hospital
2900 Sunset Boulevard
West Columbia, SC 29169
(803) 796-9911
(800) 922-1332
Intake Coordinator

Fenwick Hall Hospital
P.O. Box 688
Johns Island, SC 29455
(803) 559-2461
John H. Magil, Executive Director

New Beginnings at Fenwick Hall
P.O. Box 688-1709 River Road
Johns Island, SC 29455
(803) 559-2461
Bonnie Fargnoli

Palmetto Center
P.O. Box 5357
Florence, SC 29502
(803) 662-9378
Bob Stevens

SOUTH DAKOTA

Addiction Recovery Center
915 Mountain View Road
Rapid City, SD 57702
(605) 341-8913
James A. Dyson

Carroll Institute
304 E. Phillips, Suite 320
Sioux Falls, SD 57102
(605) 336-2556
Lorri F. Lanpher, Executive Director

Keystone Treatment Center
1010 E. 2nd Street
Canton, SD 57013
(605) 987-2751
Mitzi Carroll, Executive Director

River Park
222 S. Adams, P.O. Box 1216
Pierre, SD 57501
(605) 224-6177
Glenn L. Jorgenson

River Park Lodge
4201 S. Minnesota
Sioux Falls, SD 57105
(605) 331-2000
Sister Joyce Piatz

River Park Black Hills
Route 4, Box 1670
Rapid City, SD 57702
(605) 341-3900
Richard Keifer

Rushmore Community Health Resort
Chemical Dependency Unit
915 Mountain View
Rapid City, SD 57702
(605) 341-8913
Jim Dyson

TENNESSEE

Addiction Recovery of Chattanooga
8614 Harrison Bay Road
Harrison, TN 37341
(800) 233-3737 or
In TN (800) 821-2914
Vernon Westrich

Cumberland Heights Treatment
   Center
River Road
P.O. Box 90727
Nashville, TN 37209
(615) 352-1757
Pam Parchman, Admissions
   Coordinator

Eastwood Hospital
3000 Getwell Road
Memphis, TN 38118
(901) 369-8500
Terri Miller

HCA Indian Path Pavillion
Adult A & D Program
2300 Pavillion Drive
Kingsport, TN 37660
(615) 229-7874
Adult Program Director

HCA Parthenon Pavillion
2401 Murphy Avenue
Nashville, TN 37203
(615) 327-2237
Program Director

HCA Valley Psychiatric Hospital
   Alcohol & Drug Program
Shallowford Road,
P.O. Box 21887
Chattanooga, TN 37421
(615) 894-4220
Community Relations Director

Koala Adolescent Center
1220 Eighth Avenue
Nashville, TN 37203
(615) 726-1337
David O'Grady, D.O.C.

Koala Center of Methodist
Medical Center of Oak Ridge
990 Oak Ridge Turnpike
P.O. Box 529
Oak Ridge, TN 37830
(615) 481-1680
John Kraeder

Koala Center, Tennessee
Christian Medical Center
500 Hospital Drive
Nashville, TN 37115
(615) 868-7256
Chip Burson

Methodist Outreach, Inc.
2009 Lamar Avenue
Memphis TN 38114
(901) 276-5401
Janet Kirk

New Day Center at Scott Memorial
   Hospital
P.O. Box 747
Lawrenceburg, TN 38464
(615) 762-7501
Kirk Minor

Valley Psychiatric Hospital
P.O. Box 21887
Shallowford Road
Chattanooga, TN 37421
(615) 894-4220
John Morrison

Vita Vanderbilt University Hospital
   Chemical Dependency Programs
Medical Center, N.,
S S 440
Nashville, TN 37232
(615) 322-6158
Jane Zibelin, Program Director

TEXAS

Addiction Treatment Center
Harris Hospital HEB
2219 W. Euless Boulevard
Euless, TX 76040
(817) 267-3158
Frank Stone
Bruce London

Aldorphin Restorative Center
   Outpatient Program
437 W. Magnolia
San Antonio, TX 78212
(512) 736-5643
Kirk Middleton

Baylor-Parkside Lodge of Dallas/
   Fort Worth, Inc.
Rt. 1, Box 223AB
(Orchid Hill Lane)
Argyle, TX 76226
(817) 455-2201
Kathryn Stream

Bayview Hospital
6629 Wooldridge
Corpus Christi, TX 78415
(512) 993-9700
Ms. Ronnie Bleyer

Brookwood/Parkside Lodge
Chocolate Bayou—Houston
P.O. Box 168
638 Harbor Road
Liverpool, TX 77577
(713) 393-2023
Don Devens

Camelback Hospital
Clearview
Loop 250 and Thomason
Midland, TX 79701
(915) 697-5200
(800) 833-8080
Philip Lundberg
In Texas 1-800-592-5433

CareUnit Hopital of Dallas/Fort Worth
1066 West Magnolia Avenue
Fort Worth, TX 76104
(817) 336-2828

CareUnit Hospital Program
Baptist Hospital of South East Texas
3510 Stagg Drive
Beaumont, TX 77701
(409) 839-5387

CareUnit Hospital Program
Baylor CareUnit—Baylor
University Medical Truett
Hospital—4th Floor
3500 Gaston Avenue
Dallas, TX 75246
(214) 820-2300

CareUnit Hospital Program
Corpus Christi Osteopathic
1502 Tarlton
Corpus Christi, TX 78415
(512) 884-2524

CareUnit Hospital Program
Dallas-Fort Worth Medical Center
2709 Hospital Boulevard
Grand Prairie, TX 75051
(214) 641-5256

CareUnit Hospital Program
St. Anthony's Hospital
200 N.W. 7th Avenue
Amarillo, TX 79176-0001
(806) 378-6797

Charter Hospital of City
   View—Addiction Recovery
6201 Overton Ridge
Fort Worth, TX 76132
(817) 292-6844
Pamela J. Pohly, Director

Charter Palms Hospital
1421 E. Jackson Avenue
McAllen, TX 78501
(512) 631-5421
Fran Symore

Charter Plains Hospital
801 N. Quaker Avenue
Lubbock, TX 79416
(806) 744-5505
Admissions Office

Chemical Dependency Unit of South
   Texas
5517 S. Alameda
P.O. Box 81326
Corpus Christi, TX 78412
(512) 993-6100
Gene Hybner

Clearview—A Chemical Dependency
   Treatment Facility
P.O. Box 4757
Midland, Tx 79704
(915) 697-5200
Pam Trotta

Deer Park Hospital
4525 Glenwood Avenue
Deer Park, TX 77536
(713) 479-0955
Director of Admissions

HCA Beaumont Neurological
   Hospital—The Pinebrook Center
3250 Fannin Street
Beaumont, TX 77072
(409) 835-4921
Program Director

HCA Belle Park Hospital
4427 Belle Park Drive
Houston, TX 77072
(713) 933-6000
Director of Admissions

HCA Brazos Psychiatric
   Hospital—Chemical Dependency
   Program
P.O. Box 21446
Waco, TX 76702-1446
(817) 772-3500
Program Director

HCA Deer Park Hospital
4525 Glenwood Avenue
Deer Park, TX 77536
(713) 479-0955
Director of Admissions

HCA Houston International
   Hospital—Adult & Adolescent
   Chemical Dependency
6441 Main Street
Houston, TX 77030
(713) 795-5921
Community Relations Director

HCA Shoal Creek Hospital
Renaissance Program
3501 Mills Avenue
Austin, TX 78731
(512) 452-0361, Ext. 700

Kids of El Paso County, Inc.
P.O. Box 9069
El Paso, TX 79982
(915) 772-KIDS
J. Clauss, Intake Coordinator

Laurelwood Hospital
P.O. Box 7695
The Woodlands, TX 77387
(713) 367-4422
Phil Peterson

Live Oak Treatment Center
110 Medical Drive
Victoria, TX 77904
(512) 576-0814
(800) 582-6789
Jan Suhr

Metropolitan Hospital
Turn About Program (TAP)
7525 Scyene Road
Dallas, TX 75227
(214) 388-8261
(TELE) (214) 263-3776
Joe Green

The Oaks Recovery Center
P.O. Box 3
Denton, TX 76202
(817) 565-8135
Elaine Court, Med. CADAC

Program for Alcoholism Counseling &
   Treatment
2616 S. Loop W.
Suite 500
Houston, TX 77054
(713) 666-9811
George S. Glass, M.D.

St. Mary's Hospital
Substance Abuse Program
404 St. Mary's Boulevard
Galveston, TX 77550
(409) 766-4307
Cindy Antonelli
Program Coordinator

Starlite Village Hospital
P.O. Box 317
Center Point, TX 78010
(512) 634-2212
F.E. Seale, M.D.

Talk It Over
2515 W. Ohio Street
Midland, TX 79701
(915) 687-0531
Robert Netherland

Unit Metropolitan Hospital
7525 Scyene Road
Dallas, TX 75227
(214) 388-8261
(Tele) (214) 263-3776
Joe Green

West Oaks Hospital
6500 Hornwood Drive
Houston, TX 77074
(713) 995-0909
Nancy Tankersley

UTAH

Dayspring Utah Valley
Regional Medical Center
1034 N. 500 W.
Provo, UT 84601
(801) 375-HELP
Don Ely, Treatment Director

Highland Ridge Hospital
4578 Highland Drive
Salt Lake City, UT 84117
(801) 272-9851
(800) 321-HELP
Richard Bell, Admin.

Mountain View Hospital
Alcohol/Substance Abuse Treatment
1000 E. Highway 6
Payson, UT 84651
(801) 465-9201, Ext/412
Mike Averett, Director

VERMONT

Brattleboro Retreat
Adolescent Alcohol/Drug Program
75 Linden Street
Brattleboro, VT 05301
(802) 257-7785
Charles McLoughlin

Champlain Drug & Alcohol Services,
Inc.
45 Clarke Street
Burlington, VT 05401
(802) 862-5243
Robert Black

Founders Hall at North Eastern VT
Regional Hospital
St. Johnsbury, VT 05819
(802) 748-8141
Carol Maxwell

Howard Mental Health Services EASE
Program
300 Flynn Avenue
Burlington, VT 05401
(802) 658-0400
Chuck King

NE Kingdom Community Action
Alcohol Rehabilitation
Program—Residential
Rural Route 2
Newport, VT 05855
Isabell Glodgett
AA Meetings

NE Kingdom Mental Health
60 Broadview/Box 724
Newport, VT 05855
(802) 334-6744
Vern Barry, Substance Abuse
Program Coordinator

VIRGINIA

The Arlington Hospital
Alcoholism and Addictions
1701 N. George Mason Drive
Arlington, VA 22205
(703) 558-6536
Daniel A. Feerst, M.S.W.
Treatment Programs

Arlington Treatment Center
Route 3, Box 52
Harrisonburg, VA 22801
(703) 434-7396
Linda Deola, Program Director

Charter Westbrook Hospital
1500 Westbrook Avenue
Richmond, VA 23227
(804) 266-9671
Jean Yancey

David C. Wilson Hospital
Chemical Dependency Program
2101 Arlington Boulevard
Charlottesville, VA 22903
(804) 977-1120
Martha Sheridan

HCA Dominion Hospital
Chemical Dependency Program
2960 Sleepy Hollow Road
Falls Church, VA 22044
(703) 536-2000
Program Director

HCA Peninsula Hospital Adult
Chemical Dependency Unit
2244 Executive Drive
Hampton, VA 23666
(804) 827-1001
Program Director

HCA Roanoke Valley Psychiatric
Center
Alcohol Treatment Services
1902 Braeburn Drive
Salem, VA 24153
(703) 772-2800
Program Coordinator

Heritage-Richlands
Humana Hospital—Clinch Valley
P.O. Box 506
Richlands, VA 24641
(703) 964-9194
William Nolley, Program Director

Heritage-Richmond
Humana Hospital—St. Lukes
7700 Parham Road
Richmond, VA 23229
(804) 747-5673
Don Blakeman, Program Director

Heritage-Virginia Beach
Human Hospital—Bayside
800 Independence Boulevard
Virginia Beach, VA 23455
(804) 363-0503
Jamie Carraway

Mountain Wood
P.O. Box 5546
Charlottesville, VA 22905
(804) 971-8245
Linda Pemberton

New Beginnings at Serenity Lodge
2097 S. Military Highway
Chesapeake, VA 23320
(804) 543-6888
Judy Parker, Intake

Primavera at Culpepper
Chemical Dependency Program
P.O. Box 898
Culpepper, VA 22701
(703) 937-5133
George Swanberg

Prince William Hospital—Outpatient
  Counseling Services
9625 Surveyor Court
Suite 480
Manassas, VA 22110
(703) 369-8403
Alcice Reinke

The Ridge Street Center
210 S. Ridge Street
Danville, VA 24541
(804) 799-0456
Libby Lintz

Saint Albans Psychiatric
  Hospital—Chemical Dependency
  Program
P.O. Box 3608
Radford, VA 24143
(800) 572-3120
VA (800) 368-3468
Admissions Officer

Springwood Psychiatric Institute
Route 4, Box 50
Leesburg, VA 22075
(703) 777-0800

WASHINGTON

Awareness Express-A Youth/Adult
  Alcohol Drug Prevention &
  Treatment
614 Division Street
Port Orchard, WA 98366
(206) 876-9430
Sherry Barnhart, Director

CareUnit Hospital of Kirkland
10322 N.E. 132nd Street
Kirkland, WA 98034
(206) 821-1122

CareUnit Hospital Program
The Nancy Reagan CareUnit
Deaconess Medical Center
West 800 Fifth Avenue
Spokane, WA 92210
(509) 458-CARE

Columbia Hospital for Women, Female
  Adolescents
P.O. Box 9635
Yakima, WA 98909
(509) 865-2000
Joann Clark
Facilities for children

Forks Community Hospital
West End Outreach Service
RR No. 3, Box 3575
Forks, WA 98331
(206) 374-6177

Kairos Center
Substance Abuse Programs
100 South 1, Suite 203
Aberdeen, WA 98520
(206) 533-4940
(206) 533-2529 (24 Hrs.)
Ron Bell

Milam Recovery Centers
14500 Juanita Drive N.E.
Bothell, WA 98011
(206) 823-3116
Chuck Kester, President

New Beginnings at Lakewood General
  Hospital
5702 100th Street, S.W.
Tacoma, WA 98499-0998
(206) 582-4357
Val Vernon

Norcross Clinic
16000 Bothell/Everett Highway
Mill Creek, WA 98012
(206) 742-5233
Bill Norcross

Norcross Clinic, Inc.
209 Dayton Street
Edmonds, WA 98020
(206) 771-1194
Bill Norcross

Northwest Treatment Center
Alcohol/Drug Treatments
9010 13th N.W.
Seattle, WA 98117
(206) 789-5911
Susan Erickson, Adm. Coord.

Puyallup Tribal Treatment Center
2209 E. 32nd Street
Tacoma, WA 98404
(206) 597-6220
Leo A. Whiteford

Swarf Alcohol & Drug Programs
1104 Main Street Suite M100
Vancouver, WA 98660
(206) 693-4975
William J. Steur

Turnaround at St. Joseph
P.O. Box 1600 Fourth Floor
Vancouver, WA 98669
(206) 256-2170
Ronald Hagland, Program
Director

Whitman County Alcoholism
Chemical Dependency Program
N.E. 340 Maple Street, No. 2
Pullman, WA 99163
(509) 332-6585
Jean Iverson

WEST VIRGINIA

CareUnit Hospital Program
Charleston Area Medical Center
Brooks & Washington Street
Charleston, WV 25301
(304) 348-6200

Koala Center at South Charleston
 Community Hospital
30 MacCorkle Avenue
S. Charleston, WV 25303
(304) 744-7550
Marc Lund

WISCONSIN

Abaris Center for the Chemically
 Dependent
431 Olympian Boulevard
Beloit, WI 53511
(608) 364-1144
John McKearn

The A Center
2000 Domanik Drive
Racine, WI 53404
(414) 632-6141
Rev. E.W. Belter, D.O.

DePaul—Holy Family Chemical
 Dependency Unit
2300 Western Avenue
Manitowac, WI 54220
(800) 362-HOPE
Ann Nussey

DePaul Port Washington
743 N. Montgomery Street
Port Washington, WI 53074
(800) 242-2112
(414) 284-5872
Judy Werlein

DePaul Rehabilitation Hospital
4143 S. 13th Street
Milwaukee, WI 53221
(800) 423-6028
A. Bela Maroti, President

Dewey Center of Milwaukee
  Psychiatric Hospital
1220 Dewey Avenue
Wauwatosa, WI 53213
(414) 258-4094
(414) 258-2600
Richard Hauser, M.D.

Elmbrook Memorial Hospital
Chemical Dependency Recovery
  Center
19333 W. North Avenue
Brookfield, WI 53005
(414) 785-2233
Gene Tarwid, Director
of Clinical Services

Genesis Next Door
Foundation Substance Abuse Center
726 N. 31st Street
Milwaukee, WI 53208
(414) 931-8683
Nathan Beyer, Director

Good Shepherd Health Systems
2000 Domanik Drive
Racine, WI 53404
(800) 222-2282
Rev. E.W. Belter, D.D.

Kettle Moraine Hospital
4839 N. Hewitts Point Road
Oconomowoc, WI 53066
(414) 567-0201
Metro (414) 276-2090
Admissions Office

L.E. Phillips Treatment
2661 Country Trunk I
Chippewa Falls, WI 54729
(715) 723-5585
Lee Tiffany

Madison Family Institute
5706 Odana Road
Madison, WI 53719
(608) 271-7780
Dan Bodenz

Madison General Hospital
Newstart Program
202 S. Park Street
Madison WI 53715
(608) 267-6291
Brian M. Boegel, A.S.C.W.

McBride Center for Treatment of
  Impaired Prof. of Milwaukee
  Psychiatric Hospital
1220 Dewey Avenue
Wauwatosa, WI 53213
(414) 258-4094
(414) 258-2600
Roland Herrington, M.D.

Riverwood Center
445 Court Street North
Prescott, WI 54021
(715) 252-3286
AODA Program Director

Saint Anthony Hospital
AODA Treatment Center
1004 N. 10th Street
Milwaukee, WI 53233
(414) 271-1965
Michael Giniger

Share—Stoughton Hospital
  Association
900 Ridge Street
Stoughton, WI 53589
(608) 873-2295
Del Cornet

St. Croix Valley Hospital
Chemical Dependency Program
204 S. Adams Street
St. Croix Falls, WI 54024
(715) 483-3261
Chris Peterson

St. Francis Medical Center
700 W. Avenue S.
LaCrosse, WI 54601
(608) 785-0940
John Rosing

St. Joseph's Hospital AODA
Recovery Program
611 St. Joseph Avenue
Marshfield, WI 54449
(715) 387-9700
William R. Debartolo

Tellurian Community, Inc.
300 Femrite Drive
Madison, WI 53716
(608) 222-7311
Keith Wheeler

Theda Clark Regional Medical Center
130 2nd Street
Neenah, WI 54956
(414) 729-2037
Paul Strand

WYOMING

Powder River Council on Alcoholism
  & Drug Abuse
P.O. Box 2061
Gillette, WY 82716
(307) 686-1189
Charlotte Coppinger

II Alcoholics Anonymous Intergroups

ALABAMA
Alexander City
(205) 329-8246
Birmingham
(209) 939-1798

ALASKA
Anchorage
(907) 272-2312
Fairbanks
(907) 488-6393
Juneau
(907) 586-9476
Ketchikan
(907) 247-8711

ARIZONA
Flagstaff
(602) 526-9439
Mesa
(602) 834-9033
Peoria
(602) 979-2775
Phoenix
(602) 264-1341
Prescott
(602) 445-8691
Tucson
(602) 623-1464
Verde Valley
(602) 282-3972
Yuma
(602) 782-2605

ARKANSAS
Little Rock
(501) 372-6040

CALIFORNIA
Apple Valley
(619) 242-8812
Bakersfield
(805) 322-4025
Capitola
(408) 688-2058
Claremont
(714) 623-4415
Colton
(714) 825-4700
Eureka
(707) 442-0711

Fresno
(209) 221-6907
Fullerton
(714) 773-4357
Glendora
(818) 914-1861
Lancaster/Palmdale
(805) 948-0050
Lawndale
(213) 644-1139
Long Beach
(213) 435-5333
Los Angeles
(213) 387-8316
(213) 384-2449
(213) 474-7339
Monterey
(408) 373-3713
Napa
(707) 255-4900
Oakland
(415) 653-4300
Oxnard
(805) 487-4865
Palm Springs
(619) 323-4600
Paradise
(916) 872-1178
Pleasanton
(415) 846-9973
(415) 829-0666
Redding
(916) 246-7611
Riverside
(714) 884-8959
Sacramento
(916) 443-8138
Salinas
(408) 424-9874
San Diego
(619) 239-1365
San Fernando Valley
(818) 988-3001
San Francisco
(415) 282-3736
(415) 661-1828
San Jose
(408) 297-3555
San Mateo
(415) 573-6811
Santa Ana
(714) 556-4555

Santa Barbara
(805) 687-3989
Santa Rosa
(707) 838-2716
(707) 823-0303
Stockton
(209) 599-2328
Susanville
(916) 257-2880
Valle De San Joaquin
(209) 222-0496
Vallejo
(707) 643-8218
Vista
(714) 758-2514
Walnut Creek/Concord
(415) 939-4115

COLORADO
Colorado Springs
(303) 624-5020
Denver
(303) 322-4440
Grand Junction
(303) 245-9649
Pueblo
(303) 542-6121

CONNECTICUT
Bridgeport
(203) 333-5804
Derby
(203) 734-0312
Greenwich
(203) 869-5221
Hartford
(203) 527-1361
Stratford
(203) 847-7323

DELAWARE
Dover
(302) 736-1567
Georgetown
(302) 856-4652
Wilmington
(302) 655-5113

DISTRICT OF COLUMBIA
Washington
(202) 966-9115
(202) 797-9738

FLORIDA
Fort Lauderdale
(305) 462-9265
Fort Myers
(813) 542-6039
Islamorada
(305) 664-8683
Jacksonville
(904) 399-8537
Key West
(305) 296-8654
Largo
(813) 535-6003
Melbourne
(305) 724-2247
Miami
(305) 754-2112
New Port Richey
(813) 845-1652
New Smyrna Beach
(904) 428-4255
Panama City
(904) 785-5292
Pensacola
(904) 455-0639
Riviera Beach
(305) 844-8800
Sarasota
(813) 955-6674
Spring Hill
(904) 683-8400
Stuart
(305) 283-9337
Tampa
(813) 879-1233
Travares
(904) 343-7748
Tavernier
(305) 852-3317
Vero Beach
(305) 562-1114
Winter Park
(305) 647-3333

GEORGIA
Atlanta
(404) 525-3178
Augusta
(404) 793-5335
Brunswick
(912) 354-0993

Savannah
(912) 354-0993

HAWAII
Hilo Hawaii
(808) 961-6133
Honolulu Oahu
(808) 946-1438
Kailua-Kona, Hawaii
(808) 961-6133
Koloa Kauai
(808) 742-1562
Wailuki Maui
(808) 244-9673

IDAHO
Boise
(208) 376-1570
Coeur D'Alene
(208) 667-4714

ILLINOIS
Carbondale
(618) 549-4633
Chicago
(312) 233-3099
(312) 346-1475
(312) 252-3611
Galesburg
(309) 343-1530
Moline
(309) 764-1016
Peoria
(309) 685-2687

INDIANA
Anderson
(317) 642-2876
Elkhart
(616) 699-5338
Evansville
(812) 464-2219
Ft. Wayne
(219) 426-5721
Greensburg
(813) 663-6572
Indianapolis
(317) 632-7864
Lafayette
(317) 447-4925
Merrillville
(219) 980-3475
Muncie
(317) 747-9722
South Bend
(219) 234-7007

Terre Haute
(812) 234-0827

IOWA
Des Moines
(515) 282-8550
Dubuque
(319) 557-9197
Sioux City
(712) 252-1333

KANSAS
Ulysses
(316) 356-3003
Wichita
(316) 684-3661

KENTUCKY
Covington
(606) 491-7181
Lexington
(606) 255-4393
Louisville
(502) 582-1849

LOUISIANA
Baton Rouge
(504) 924-0030
Lafayette
(318) 234-7814
Many
(318) 256-3375
New Orleans
(504) 525-1178
Opelousas
(318) 585-6833
Shreveport
(318) 227-8170

MAINE
Portland
(207) 774-3034

MARYLAND
Aberdeen
(301) 272-4150
Annapolis
(301) 268-5441
Baltimore
(301) 467-4667
Easton
(301) 822-4226
Hughesville
(800) 492-0209

Rockville
(301) 251-1024
Salisbury
(301) 749-1476
Thurmont
(301) 791-2687

MASSACHUSETTS
Boston
(617) 426-9444
Holyoke
(413) 532-2111
Hyannis
(617) 775-7060
Worcester
(617) 752-9000

MICHIGAN
Ann Arbor
(313) 663-6225
Bay City
(517) 894-4208
Detroit
(313) 962-9191
Ferndale
(313) 541-6565
Greenville
(616) 754-6684
Lansing
(517) 325-8781
Monroe
(313) 243-5163
Mt. Morris
(313) 687-2031
Pontiac
(313) 332-3521

MINNESOTA
Duluth
(218) 728-5572
Minneapolis
(612) 874-1447
St. Paul
(612) 776-6566

MISSISSIPPI
Jackson
(601) 354-2136

MISSOURI
Kansas City
(816) 471-4606

Springfield
(417) 866-2349
St. Charles
(314) 723-6965
St. Louis
(314) 371-1432
(314) 353-5353
(314) 647-3677

MONTANA
Billings
(406) 248-2042
Great Falls
(406) 452-1234
Havre
(406) 265-1152
Helena
(406) 442-3366
Missoula
(406) 721-6084
Sidney
(406) 482-5080
Whitefish
(406) 892-3839

NEVADA
Las Vegas
(702) 732-4007
Reno
(702) 329-7593

NEBRASKA
Lincoln
(402) 466-5214
Omaha
(402) 345-9916

NEW HAMPSHIRE
Manchester
(603) 622-6967
Portsmouth
(603) 436-8001

NEW JERSEY
Atlantic City
(609) 927-6825
Cherry Hill
(609) 428-4482
Maplewood
(201) 763-1415
Newark
(201) 770-0725
Summers Point
(609) 927-3509
Trenton
(609) 393-8010

NEW MEXICO
Albuquerque
(505) 881-1900
Gallup
(505) 722-4818
Santa Fe
(505) 988-2947

NEW YORK
Albany
(518) 489-6779
Buffalo
(716) 853-0388
Ithaca
(607) 273-1541
Lake Huntington
(914) 932-8955
New York
(212) 473-6200
Newburgh
(914) 342-5757
Niagara Falls
(716) 283-0368
Rochester
(716) 232-6720
Smithtown
(516) 654-1124
Syracuse
(315) 422-1802
W. Hempstead
(516) 794-1144

NORTH CAROLINA
Asheville
(704) 254-8539
Charlotte
(704) 332-4387
Greensboro
(919) 292-6806
Wilmington
(919) 763-2151

NORTH DAKOTA
Fargo
(701) 293-0291

OHIO
Akron
(216) 253-8181
Cincinnati
(513) 861-4211
Cleveland
(216) 241-7387
Columbus
(614) 253-8501
Dayton
(513) 222-2211

Mansfield
(419) 526-9524
Newark
(614) 345-7060
Sandusky
(419) 625-5995
Toledo
(419) 472-8242
Youngstown
(216) 744-1935

OKLAHOMA
Oklahoma City
(405) 524-1100
Tulsa
(918) 743-4474

OREGON
Corvallis
(503) 753-7508
Eugene
(503) 342-4113
La Grande
(503) 963-6437
Portland
(503) 223-8569
Salem
(503) 399-0599
Siletz
(503) 265-8302

PENNSYLVANIA
Altoona
(814) 943-3147
Mercer
(412) 342-0162
Philadelphia
(215) 545-4023
Pittsburgh
(412) 471-7472
Reading
(215) 373-6500
Tarentum
(412) 226-3203
York
(717) 854-4617

PUERTO RICO
Comerio
(809) 875-2790
Santurce
(809) 781-3223

RHODE ISLAND
Providence
(401) 438-8860

Warwick
(401) 739-8777

SOUTH CAROLINA
Columbia
(803) 254-5301
Myrtle Beach
(803) 448-2546
Taylor
(803) 244-1830

SOUTH DAKOTA
Sioux Falls
(605) 338-6800

TENNESSEE
Chattanooga
(615) 265-9001
Knoxville
(615) 522-9667
Memphis
(901) 454-1414
Nashville
(615) 298-1050

TEXAS
Austin
(512) 451-8251
Brownsville
(512) 542-4874
Corpus Christi
(512) 853-0234
Dallas
(214) 631-1675
El Paso
(915) 562-4081
Fort Worth
(817) 332-3533
Houston
(713) 772-7214
Nederland
(409) 724-6501
San Angelo
(915) 655-5641
San Antonio
(512) 733-7562
Tyler
(214) 561-3681
Waco
(817) 754-3336

UTAH
Ogden
(801) 393-4728
Provo
(801) 375-8620
Richmond
(801) 258-5157

Salt Lake City
(801) 484-7871

VIRGINIA
Charlottesville
(804)293-6565
Falls Church
(703) 577-9587
(703) 241-8195
Harrisonburg
(703) 434-8870
Lynchburg
(804) 847-7826
Newport News
(804) 874-7037
Richmond
(804) 262-5865
Staunton
(703) 885-6912
Virginia Beach
(804) 490-3980
Winchester
(703) 667-0322

WASHINGTON
Bellevue
(206) 454-9192
Kennewick
(509) 586-9714
McMillan
(206) 841-4158
Olympia
(206) 352-7344
Seattle
(206) 323-3606
Spokane
(509) 624-1442
Tacoma
(206) 272-2448
Vancouver
(206) 694-3870
Yakima
(509) 575-9945

WISCONSIN
Green Bay
(414) 432-7494
Kenosha
(414) 654-8246
Lacrosse
(608) 784-7560
Madison
(608) 244-8414
Milwaukee
(414) 272-3081
Plover
(715) 344-4042

WYOMING
Cheyenne
(307) 632-4995

ALBERTA
Calgary
(403) 233-2111
Edmonton
(403) 482-6783
Fort McMurray
(403) 743-0099
Lethbridge
(403) 329-0591
Medicine Hat
(403) 527-7953

BRITISH COLUMBIA
Chilliwack
(604) 792-1461
Dawson Creek
(604) 782-4733

Kamloops
(604) 554-1920
Nanaimo
(604) 753-7513
Prince George
(604) 562-4049
Sydney
(604) 656-2056
Vancouver
(604) 873-8466
Vernon
(604) 545-4933

MANITOBA
Winnipeg
(204) 233-3508

NEWFOUNDLAND
Gander
(709) 651-2001
St. John's
(709) 579-5215

NOVA SCOTIA
Halifax
(902) 422-5875

ONTARIO
Barrie
(705) 728-6581
Elliot Lake
(705) 461-3150
Hamilton
(416) 529-2104
London
(519) 438-1122
North Bay
(705) 474-7940
Ottawa
(613) 523-9977
Peterborough
(709) 745-6111
Sault Ste. Marie
(705) 254-1312
St. Catharines
(416) 688-2797

St. Thomas
(519) 633-2127
Sudbury
(705) 566-8053
Thunder Bay
(807) 344-1712
Toronto
(416) 487-5591

QUEBEC
Laurent
(514) 894-0487
Montreal
(418) 681-5775
(514) 273-7544

SASKATCHEWAN
Regina
(306) 352-7500
Saskatoon
(306) 665-6272
Swift Current
(306) 773-2632

III   Al-Anon or Alateen

Al-Anon/Alateen
World Service Office
P.O. Box 862
Midtown Station
New York, New York 10018-
0862

IV   State Authorities

ALABAMA
Alcoholism Program
Department of Mental
Health
200 Interstate Pk. Dr.
Box 3710
Montgomery, AL 36193
(205) 271-9253

ALASKA
Office of Alcoholism and
Drug Abuse
Pouch H-05F
Juneau, AK 99811
(907) 586-6201

ARIZONA
Alcohol Abuse Section
Division of Behavioral
Health Services

2500 E. Van Buren Street
Phoenix, AZ 85008
(602) 255-1238

CALIFORNIA
Department of Alcohol and
Drug Programs
111 Capitol Mall
Sacramento, CA 95814
(916) 445-1940

COLORADO
Colorado Department of
Health
Alcohol & Drug Abuse
Division
4210 East 11th Avenue
Denver, CO 80220
(303) 320-6137

CONNECTICUT
Connecticut Alcohol and
Drug Abuse Commission
999 Asylum Avenue
3rd Floor
Hartford, CT 06105
(203) 566-2089

DELAWARE
Alcoholism Services
Lower Kensington
Environmental Center
1910 N. Dupont Highway
New Castle, DE 19720
(302) 421-6111

DISTRICT OF COLUMBIA
Alcoholism and Drug Abuse
Administration Central
Office

1875 Connecticut Avenue,
Ste. 837
Washington, DC 20009

FLORIDA
Alcohol & Drug Abuse
Program
Department of Health &
Rehab
1317 Winewood Boulevard
Tallahassee, FL 32301
(904) 488-0900

GEORGIA
Alcohol and Drug Abuse
Service Station
878 Peachtree Street
Ste. 319
Atlanta, GA 30309
(404) 894-4785

HAWAII
Alcohol and Drug Abuse
Branch
PO Box 3378
Honolulu, HI 96801
(808) 548-4280

IDAHO
Substance Abuse Section
Health & Welfare
Department
450 W. State Street
Boise, ID 83720
(208) 334-4368

ILLINOIS
Department of Mental
Health & Developmental
Disabilities
902 S. Wind Road
Springfield, IL 62703
(217) 786-6314

INDIANA
Division of Addiction
Services
429 N. Pennsylvania Street
Indianapolis, IN 46204
(317) 232-7816

IOWA
Iowa Dept. of Substance
Abuse
507 10th Street, Ste. 500

Des Moines, IA 50319
(515) 281-3641

KANSAS
Kansas Alcohol & Drug
Abuse Services Dept. of
Social & Rehab
Biddle Bldg.
2700 W. 6th Street
Topeka, KS 66606
(913) 296-3925

KENTUCKY
Division of Substance Abuse
Dept. for MHMR Services
275 E. Main Street
Frankfort, KY 40621
(502) 564-2880

LOUISIANA
Office of Prevention &
Recovery from Alcohol &
Drug Abuse
PO Box 53129
Baton Rouge, LA 70892
(504) 922-0728

MAINE
Office of Alcoholism and
Drug Abuse Prevention
State House Stn. 11
Augusta, ME 04333
(207) 289-2781

MARYLAND
Alcoholism Control
Administration
201 SW Preston Street
4th Floor
Baltimore, MD 21202
(301) 383-2781

MASSACHUSETTS
Division of Alcoholism
150 Tremont Street
Boston, MA 02111
(617) 727-1960

MICHIGAN
Office of Substance Abuse
Services
Dept. of Public Health
3500 N. Logan
Lansing, MI 48914
(517) 373-8600

MINNESOTA
Chemical Dependency

Prog. Division
Dept. of Human Services
444 Lafayette Road
St. Paul, MN 55101
(612) 296-3991

MISSISSIPPI
Division of Alcohol & Drug
Abuse
1102 Robert E. Lee Bldg.
Jackson, MS 39201
(601) 359-1297

MISSOURI
Division of Alcohol & Drug
Abuse
Dept. of Mental Health
2002 Missouri Boulevard
Jefferson City, MO 65101
(314) 751-4942

MONTANA
Department of Institutions
Alcohol & Drug Abuse
Division
1539 11th Avenue
Helena, MT 59620
(406) 444-2827

NEBRASKA
Division of Alcoholism and
Drug Abuse
Box 94728
Lincoln, NE 68509
(402) 471-2851

NEVADA
Bureau of Alcohol & Drug
Abuse
505 King Street—
Kinkead Bldg. 500
Carson City, NV 89701
(702) 885-4790

NEW HAMPSHIRE
New Hampshire Office of
A & D Abuse Prevention
H & W Bldg., Hazen Drive
Concord, NH 03301
(603) 271-4627

NEW JERSEY
Division of Alcoholism
CN 362
Trenton, NJ 08625
(609) 292-8947

NEW MEXICO
Alcoholism Bureau

Behavioral Health
Services Division
PO Box 968
Santa Fe, NM 87504
(505) 984-0020

NEW YORK
NYC Division of Alcoholism
& Alcohol Abuse
194 Washington Avenue
Albany, NY 12210
(518) 474-3377

Odyssey House Inc.
309 East 6th Street
New York, New York 10003
(212) 477-9633
(212) 477-9634
Admissions

Phoenix House Foundation
Inc.
164 West 74th Street
New York, New York 10023
(212) 595-5810
Admissions and Information

NORTH CAROLINA
Alcohol and Drug Abuse
Services
Division of Human
Resources
325 N. Salisbury Street
Raleigh, NC 27611
(919) 829-4670

NORTH DAKOTA
Division of Alcoholism &
Drug Abuse Dept. of
Human Services
Judicial Wing 3d Floor
Capitol
Bismarck, ND 58505
(701) 224-2769

OHIO
Bureau on Alcohol Abuse
and Alcoholism Recovery
170 N. High Street, 3rd Floor
Columbus, OH 43215
(614) 466-3445

OKLAHOMA
Department of Mental
Health
Programs Division
PO Box 53277 Capitol
Station

Oklahoma City, OK 73105
(405) 521-0044

OREGON
Programs for Alcohol and
Drug Problems
301 Public Service Bldg.
Salem, OR 97310
(503) 378-2163

PENNSYLVANIA
PA Dept. of Health
Office of D&A Programs
PO Box 90
Harrisburg, PA 17108
(717) 787-9857

RHODE ISLAND
Division of Substance Abuse
Detoxification Unit
412 Howard Avenue—
Ben Rush Bldg.
Cranston, RI 02920
(401) 464-2531

SOUTH CAROLINA
South Carolina Commission
on Alcohol and Drug
Abuse
3700 Forest Drive, Ste. 300
Columbia, SC 29204
(803) 758-2521

SOUTH DAKOTA
State Department of Health
Division of Alcohol & Drug
Abuse
Joe Foss Bldg. 523 E. Capitol
Pierre, SD 57501-3182
(605) 773-3123

TENNESSEE
Tennessee Dept. of Mental
Health
Division of A&D Abuse
Services
505 Deaderick Street
4th Floor
Nashville, TN 37219
(615) 741-1921

TEXAS
Commission on Alcoholism
1705 Guadalupe

Austin, TX 78701
(512) 475-2577

UTAH
Division of Alcoholism &
Drugs
PO Box 45500
150 SW N. Temple 350
Salt Lake City
UT 84145-0500
(801) 533-6532

VERMONT
Office of Alcohol and Drug
Abuse Programs
103 S. Main Street
Waterbury, VT 05676
(802) 241-2170

VIRGINIA
Office of Substance Abuse
Department of Mental
Health
PO Box 1797
Richmond, VA 23214
(804) 786-1524

WASHINGTON
Office on Alcoholism Dept.
of Social and Health
Services
Mail Stop OB-44W
Olympia, WA 98504
(206) 753-5866

WEST VIRGINIA
Division on Alcoholism &
Drug Abuse
West Virginia Dept. of
Health
1800 Washington Street E.
Charleston, WV 25305
(304) 348-2276

WISCONSIN
Office of Alcohol & Other
Drug Abuse
1 W. Wilson Street
PO Box 7851
Madison, WI 53707
(608) 266-2717

WYOMING
Substance Abuse Division of
Community Programs
State Office Bldg.
Cheyenne, WY 82002
(307) 777-7115

INDEX